THE HIDDEN PSALMS OF DAVID

By King David

ISBN: 9798241127037

Contents

INTRODUCTION 4

CHAPTER I – The Shepherd's First Song: Before the Crown, Before the War 15

CHAPTER II – The Harp That Calmed a King's Madness 23

CHAPTER III – The Psalm Sung to the Stars Above Bethlehem 29

CHAPTER IV – The Song of the Hidden Lion: Courage Before Goliath 36

CHAPTER V – The Blood-Red Psalm: After the Giant Fell 41

CHAPTER VI – The Song Saul Was Never Meant to Hear 46

CHAPTER VII – The Psalm of the Broken Cave: When the Anointed Was Hunted 55

CHAPTER VIII – The Song of the Loyal Warrior: Jonathan's Secret Covenant 64

CHAPTER IX – The Wilderness Lament: Forty Nights Without a Throne 71

CHAPTER X – The Song of the Crown Laid Down in Tears 78

CHAPTER XI – The Psalm of the Dancing King 86

CHAPTER XII – The Song of Silent Guilt: Before Bathsheba Was Seen 94

CHAPTER XIII – The Psalm Born from Adultery and Fire 102

CHAPTER XIV – The Song of the Prophet's Finger: When Nathan Spoke 111

CHAPTER XV – The Psalm of Ashes and Repentance .. 120

CHAPTER XVI – The Song of the Child Who Did Not Live 130

CHAPTER XVII – The Psalm of a Father Betrayed 140

CHAPTER XIX – The Psalm of the Broken Throne 150

CHAPTER XX – The Song of the Oak Tree and the Hanging Prince 161

CHAPTER XXI – The Psalm of the King Who Refused to Kill Saul 171

CHAPTER XXII – The Song of the Warrior Who Laid Down the Sword 181

CHAPTER XXIII – The Psalm of White Hair and Lingering Fire 191

CHAPTER XXIV – The Song of the House That He Was Not Allowed to Build 200

CHAPTER XXV – The Psalm of the Final Anointing 211

CHAPTER XXVI – The Song of the King Who Gave His Throne to Solomon 221

CHAPTER XXVII – The Final Psalm Whispered on the Edge of Death 231

CHAPTER XXVIII – The Eternal Song: The Voice of David That Still Heals the World 240

INTRODUCTION

The Songs That Were Never Meant to Be Silenced

Before David became a king,
before he became a warrior,
before history carved his name into stone,
he was a **voice in the wilderness**.

A boy beneath vast skies.
A shepherd among silent hills.
A soul learning how to speak with God
before learning how to speak with men.

This book is not about the David of monuments.
Not the David of military triumphs.
Not the David carved into stained glass and sermons.

This book is about the **hidden David**—
the one who trembled in lonely fields,
who sang when no one listened,
who broke before he conquered,
who learned God before he learned power.

These are not the Psalms you know.
These are the **psalms that lived in his chest before they lived on parchment**.
The songs that never reached temple choirs.
The cries that dissolved into the night air.
The whispers spoken when even angels seemed distant.

This is the **Book of the Unheard Voice**.

The Boy Who Learned God in the Dark

Long before armor ever warmed his skin,
David learned the weight of the stars.

He learned it on cold stone.
On lonely ridges.
With sheep as witnesses and the wind as the only audience.

No crown shimmered above him then.
No army waited at his back.
No prophet had yet named him chosen.

Yet heaven was already listening.

There are souls who meet God in temples.
And there are souls who meet God where nothing else exists.

David was the second kind.

In the wilderness,
there are no distractions.
Only fear.
Only silence.
Only truth.

And into that truth,
David learned to sing.

Not to perform.
Not to impress.
Not to be remembered.

But to survive.

His first psalms were not theology.
They were **breaths shaped into sound**.
They were what the heart does
when the mouth cannot hold despair anymore.

When wolves circled.
When rain punished the hills.
When loneliness became heavier than hunger.

David sang.

And the heavens tilted closer.

Why These Psalms Were Never Written

Not every holy thing is meant for scripture.

Some revelations are too raw.
Too personal.
Too dangerous for religion.

The Bible recorded David's glory.
But these psalms carry his **naked soul**.

They speak of:

- Fear that faith did not immediately silence
- Desire that prayer did not immediately undo
- Rage that repentance had not yet softened
- Guilt that tore deeper than judgment
- Love that restraint transformed into fire

These psalms were not organized.

They erupted.

They bled.

They surfaced in caves,
in exile,
in betrayal,
in the smell of blood,
in the ache of longing for what could not be taken.

They were never sung in the Temple
because some songs are meant only
for the ears of God.

The David Who Terrifies the Religious

Religion prefers polished saints.
David was never polished.

He was alive.

He doubted.
He failed.
He desired.
He destroyed.
He wept like a child and commanded like a storm.

If David had lived in our age,
many would cancel him.

Others would idolize him.
Few would understand him.

Because the truth is uncomfortable:

God did not choose David because he was pure.
God chose David because he was real.

These hidden psalms reveal that reality.

They show us a man who did not approach God as an institution—
but as a **desperate listener approaching fire**.

The Songs That Healed Before They Ruled

Before David ruled a nation,
his songs ruled his chaos.

Before he commanded armies,
his voice commanded his own fear.

Before he judged nations,
his psalms judged his own heart.

We live in a world that rewards noise.
David lived in a world that rewarded listening.

These psalms are not weapons.
They are **medicine**.

They heal:

- The wound of abandonment
- The terror of being unseen
- The shame of falling after calling
- The ache of loving without possessing
- The loneliness of leadership
- The terror of becoming what you once feared

These are psalms for the people
who no longer trust easy faith.

For those who believe in God
but are tired of pretending to be flawless.

For those who still sing—
quietly—
so their doubt doesn't hear them.

Why This Book Exists Now

David lived in a violent age.
We live in a shattered one.

He fought giants of stone and bronze.
We fight giants of emptiness, confusion, despair,
identity, meaning.

Yet the battlefield is the same:

The human heart.

These psalms return now
because humanity is again wandering in caves—

Caves of isolation.
Caves of addiction.
Caves of numbness.
Caves of anxiety.
Caves of borrowed identities.

And just as before,
God still listens for a voice in the dark.

What These Psalms Will Not Do

This book will not entertain you.

It will not flatter you.

It will not give you easy answers.

It will not make you feel religious.

It will not protect you from yourself.

What These Psalms Will Do

They will:

- Break your fake strength
- Expose your hidden wars
- Teach you how to stand without armor
- Teach you how to kneel without shame
- Teach you how to fail without vanishing
- Teach you how to repent without self-hatred
- Teach you how to love without consuming
- Teach you how to suffer without becoming bitter

They will not make you powerful.

They will make you **true**.

And truth is more dangerous than power.

The Secret of David's Power

David did not become powerful because he was fearless.

He became powerful because he allowed fear
to teach him how to kneel.

He did not conquer because he was violent.

He conquered because he learned
how to obey what was greater than instinct.

He did not become holy because he never sinned.

He became holy because he **never hid from God**.

Even when he hid from people.

A Warning to the Reader

If you read this book casually,
it will pass through you like dust.

If you read it emotionally,
it will trouble you.

If you read it honestly,
it will change you.

Because these psalms do not seek attention.

They seek **alignment**.

And alignment is never comfortable at first.

The Invitation

You hold now
the unheard cries of a shepherd,
the trembling faith of a hunted man,
the repentant tears of a fallen king,
and the final whispers of a soul
learning how to die in peace.

These are not religious artifacts.

They are **human warfare songs**
written against:

Fear.
Shame.
Power addiction.
Spiritual arrogance.
Despair.
Loneliness.
Identity collapse.

Before You Enter Chapter One

Do not read these psalms as stories.

Read them as **mirrors**.

David is not your hero here.

He is your reflection.

And if you dare to listen deeply enough,
you may discover that:

You, too, have been singing in the dark
without realizing heaven was listening.

CHAPTER I – The Shepherd's First Song: Before the Crown, Before the War

Before David was known to anyone beyond the hills of Bethlehem, before his name would travel on the lips of soldiers, priests, and kings, he was simply a boy among sheep. Not a remarkable boy in the eyes of men. He owned no weapons, no inheritance of power, no promise of fame. His hands were rough from stones and wool, his feet hardened by paths no one cared to map. The house he came from was modest, crowded with brothers stronger, taller, louder than him. In that household, David was the smallest voice—and for that reason, often the last to be heard.

Jesse, his father, loved him, but did not understand him. Like most fathers, he valued what he could measure: strength in the arms, boldness in speech, obedience without questions. David was obedient, yes—but his obedience was quiet, inward, filled with wondering. While his brothers competed and dreamed of glory, David wandered the edges of fields and spoke to the sky as if it were listening.

And in truth—it was.

The days of shepherding were long and silent. The sheep moved slowly, endlessly chewing, endlessly drifting. The sun ruled everything. At dawn it was gentle, at noon merciless, and by evening it softened again as if repenting for what it had done. David walked behind the flock with a staff in one hand and stones in his pouch. Wolves were a danger, lions a rumor, thieves a possibility. But loneliness was constant.

It was during those long stretches of nothing that the first song was born.

At first, David did not know he was singing. It began as breath—slow, steady breathing to fight the fear that came when darkness fell and the fields grew strange. Then the breath became sound. Low at first. Almost embarrassed to exist. A note without words. A trembling of the voice that surprised even him.

He stopped walking.

The sheep continued. The wind moved through the grass.

David listened to his own voice fading into the open sky. Something inside his chest stirred in a way he had never felt before. It was not pride. It was not excitement. It was recognition—like finding a door inside himself that had never been opened.

So he sang again.

This time the sound was stronger. Still wordless. Still uncertain. But truer.

Night after night, the voice returned. Sometimes trembling. Sometimes breaking. Sometimes steady like a river at rest. David began shaping it into words. Simple words at first. Questions more than declarations.

"Are You there?"

"Do You see this place?"

"Do You see me?"

He did not yet call the Eternal by name. He simply spoke into the darkness as if something—or Someone— might be standing just beyond the circle of his small fire.

And something was listening.

He began to notice that after he sang, fear loosened its grip. The shadows did not retreat, but they stopped feeling hostile. Even the animals seemed to settle. The sheep gathered closer, breathing slow and heavy. The night no longer felt empty. It felt occupied.

David did not understand what was happening. He only knew that when he sang, he was no longer alone.

One night, a storm came without warning. The sky darkened violently, clouds rolling like war drums above the hills. Rain struck the ground in harsh, drenching sheets. The sheep panicked, scattering in all directions. David ran through mud and water, shouting, slipping, dragging frightened animals back together. Thunder split the sky so close it felt as though the earth itself had torn open.

By the time the storm calmed, David was soaked, shaking, bruised from falling on hidden stones. His fire was gone. His hands were numb. The sheep huddled tightly around him in the cold.

And that was when despair came for the first time.

Not fear. Not loneliness.

Despair.

The heavy kind that whispers that nothing matters, that the dark is stronger than effort, that the sky does not care who you are.

David sat in the mud and felt the weight of it press into his chest. For the first time, he did not want to sing.

The silence grew thick around him.

Then, without planning it, without deciding it, he spoke aloud—not as a song, not even as a prayer yet:

"If You are real… You have to be here now."

His voice cracked as he said it.

No thunder answered. No fire fell. No angels appeared.

But something shifted.

Not outside.

Inside.

David felt the urge to breathe deeply. Then again. Then he began to hum—not because he felt strong, but because he felt weak enough to need help. The hum turned into broken words. The broken words turned into a plea. The plea turned into a first true psalm of his life:

"You are higher than this storm.
You are closer than this fear.
If I fall here, You fall with me.
If I stand, You stand within me."

The rain slowed.

The sheep stilled.

And inside David, something aligned.

He did not become brave that night.

He became connected.

From that point on, the songs changed. They were no longer only questions. They became conversations. Arguments. Confessions. Accusations. Gratitude. Rage. Trust. Failure. Hope. Longing.

He sang when lions appeared in the distance.
He sang when wolves circled the flock.
He sang when hunger knotted his stomach.
He sang when his brothers mocked him.
He sang when his father forgot him in the fields while the family gathered for sacrifice.

And through every song, something invisible grew stronger.

Not his fame.
Not his power.
Not his skill.

His alignment.

The animals noticed it before people ever would. Predators hesitated when he stood his ground. Not because he was dangerous, but because he was unafraid to stand alone. Fear still existed in him—but it no longer ruled him.

Eventually, David learned to carry a harp. The strings felt unnatural under his fingers at first. Callused hands were not made for delicate motion. But the moment the first true chord sounded, something old and sacred woke up inside him. The harp did not replace his voice. It magnified it.

Sound became prayer.

Prayer became shelter.

Shelter became identity.

Years later, men would say David had been born for war. That he was destined for blood and command and crowns. They would say this because they could not see what had shaped him before the battlefield.

Before the giant.

Before the crown.

Before the sword.

David had already learned how to kneel in the dark without collapsing.

He had already learned how to trust without proof.

He had already learned how to stand alone and speak to the unseen.

That was his real training.

Not with weapons.
Not with tactics.
Not with banners.

With silence.

With fear.

With song.

And with a God who chose to listen to a lonely shepherd before listening to a king.

The wars would come later.
The victories would come later.
The failures would come later.
The crown would come later.

But the most important battle of David's life had already begun in a field no one remembered.

And he had already learned how to sing inside it.

CHAPTER II – The Harp That Calmed a King's Madness

The Hidden Power of Anointed Music

Madness does not always announce itself with screams.

Sometimes it arrives quietly.

Sometimes it settles into the mind like a shadow that refuses to move with the sun. It twists what is familiar into something threatening. It turns sleep into a battlefield. It transforms power into fear wearing armor.

That is how it came for King Saul.

At first, no one dared to name it. He was the anointed king of Israel—tall, commanding, once fearless. The same man who had been chosen by God in front of the people now paced his chambers at night like a hunted animal. His temper flared without warning. His eyes grew distant, then wild. At times, he would stare at the walls as if voices whispered from inside the stone.

The priests said it was exhaustion.
The generals said it was pressure.
The court said it was nothing at all.

But the servants knew better.

They heard him screaming in the night.

They saw him grip his spear during feasts as if invisible enemies surrounded him. They watched him turn on loyal men with suspicion, then beg forgiveness with tears hours later. His soul swung between fury and despair like a door in a storm.

Something was breaking inside the king.

And no one could stop it.

Until someone remembered the shepherd.

David's name drifted into the court not as a warrior, not as a hero—but as a rumor.

"There is a boy," one servant said hesitantly, "who plays as if the air itself obeys him."

Another added, "When he sings, fear leaves the room."

Saul did not believe such talk. He had no patience for mysticism. But when the darkness tightened around his mind one night so brutally that he clawed at his own arms, he finally shouted:

"Bring him."

And so David was taken from the fields.

The journey to the palace felt unreal. One morning he awoke with sheep and dust and ordinary silence. By evening he stood before towering stone, bronze gates, and guards whose eyes measured him as if he were a threat and a curiosity at the same time.

Inside, the palace felt heavy. Not with gold. With tension.

David felt it immediately. The air inside Saul's dwelling was thick, restless, charged with something wounded and dangerous. He clutched his harp tighter than he ever had.

When they brought him before the king, Saul did not rise. He sat slouched on his throne, fingers gripping the armrest too tightly. His gaze snapped toward the boy like a blade drawn too fast.

"So," Saul said sharply, "you are the shepherd."

David swallowed. "Yes, my lord."

"You are supposed to drive demons with strings?"

David did not answer with theology. He answered with truth.

"I only play, my lord. What leaves… leaves on its own."

Saul laughed bitterly. "Then play."

David sat where they indicated. His hands trembled as he placed them on the strings. The room was crowded—priests, guards, servants, advisors—but it felt emptier than any field he had ever known.

And inside Saul, the storm gathered.

David closed his eyes.

He did not think of notes.

He thought of the night rain.
The cold mud.
The fear.
The voice that had answered without lightning.

And he began to play.

At first, the music sounded uncertain, thin as a fragile thread. Saul sneered slightly, breathing heavy, his foot tapping in agitation. But David continued. His fingers found patterns his mind had never rehearsed. The music deepened. It slowed.

Something inside the sound began to descend.

The guards shifted uncomfortably. The servants stilled. One by one, conversations ceased.

And Saul stopped breathing so fast.

The melody did not attack the darkness in him. It did not argue with it. It did not shame it. It simply surrounded it—like water around a burning thing.

For the first time in months, the voices in Saul's mind fell quiet.

His fingers loosened from the throne.
His shoulders dropped slightly.
His eyes softened with confusion.

"What is this?" he whispered.

David did not answer.

He continued.

And inside Saul, something ancient began to remember peace.

When the final note faded, silence remained—but it was no longer violent. It was wide. Gentle. Almost holy.

Saul exhaled.

The room released its breath.

"Play again," the king said quietly.

From that night on, David was summoned again and again. Whenever the darkness returned, the harp was brought. And each time, the madness retreated—not destroyed, but disarmed.

Saul did not understand why.

But the Spirit did.

David was not healing Saul with sound.

He was healing him with alignment.

The difference between distraction and deliverance is truth.

David's music was not entertainment. It was prayer without language. It bypassed Saul's defenses and spoke directly to the wounded throne inside him.

Yet the madness was not gone.

It watched.
It waited.

And slowly... it learned David's name.

At first, Saul treated the boy like a remedy. Then like a possession. Then—without realizing it—like a threat.

Because the darkness always fears what can calm it.

And somewhere deep inside the king's tortured mind, a terrible suspicion was forming:

If this shepherd holds peace in his hands…
Then what else might he one day hold?

David sensed none of this. He was still a boy. He still believed that healing meant safety. That relief meant friendship. That calm meant trust.

He did not yet know that the same music that gentled the king would one day awaken the king's deepest terror.

But for now, the harp still ruled the night.

And for the first time in a long time,
Saul could sleep.

CHAPTER III – The Psalm Sung to the Stars Above Bethlehem

When the Heavens First Answered a Boy's Voice

The palace had walls thick as mountains, but David never slept well inside them.

Stone can keep out wolves and enemies, but it cannot keep out silence. And the silence of the palace was not the kind he knew from the fields. The silence of Bethlehem had been wide, alive, filled with wind, insects, distant hills breathing in the dark. The silence of the palace was heavy, trapped, watching.

So whenever Saul's madness loosened its grip for a night, whenever the king slept without thrashing or shouting, David slipped away.

No one stopped him. He was only the harp boy. Invisible unless needed.

He crossed corridors lit by oil lamps, passed sleeping guards, stepped through gates meant for warriors and kings—and climbed alone onto the highest terrace of the palace.

From there, the world opened again.

Bethlehem lay in the darkness beyond the hills, quiet and humble. And above it all stretched the sky—vast, endless, untouched by human fear. David lifted his face to the stars, and his chest loosened. This was the silence he knew. This was the silence that listened.

That night, something inside him was restless.

Not afraid.

Not sorrowful.

Restless in the way a seed stirs beneath soil when rain is near.

He had calmed a king with his music.

That frightened him.

Because power had brushed against him, and he did not yet know what power could become.

So he did what he had always done when confusion pressed against his ribs.

He sang.

Not softly.

Openly.

To the sky.

He did not sing as a servant, or as a healer, or as a court musician. He sang as the shepherd boy the stars had known long before the palace did.

"O Watcher of all paths," he whispered first, testing the air with sound,
"You who hung these fires in blackness—
do You see me still?"

The stars did not move.

But something inside him leaned upward.

His voice grew steadier.

"I am no king. I own no land.
My hands are small before Your storms.
Yet I have calmed a throne with breath.
Tell me why."

The night deepened.

The wind stirred across the terrace like a quiet witness. David felt the strange sensation he had felt before in the fields—the feeling that his words were not dissolving into emptiness, but traveling. Being received.

So he continued.

"If You give me strength, teach me mercy.
If You give me favor, teach me fear.
If You lift me up, do not let me forget the dust."

And for the first time in his life, the sky answered.

Not with thunder.

Not with flame.

But with presence.

The stars seemed… nearer.

Not physically closer—but suddenly intimate. As if the distance between his small voice and the vast heavens had folded inward on itself. David's breath caught. His hands trembled.

He no longer felt like a boy singing upward.

He felt like a boy standing *inside* something immense.

His voice broke unintentionally as the first true psalm of calling tore out of him:

"The heavens know my name.
The dark does not consume me.
Even if my feet walk where I did not choose—
You walk within my path."

Tears slid down his face—not from sadness, but from overwhelming nearness. He dropped to his knees on the cold stone, clutching the edge of the terrace as if gravity itself had shifted.

The stars burned quietly.

And something ancient locked into place inside his soul.

This was not comfort.

This was appointment.

David did not yet have language for it, but he felt it all the same:
His voice was no longer only a refuge.

It was a summons.

From that night on, his songs changed again.

Before, his psalms had been survival.
Then they became healing.

Now they became **direction**.

He began to feel—faintly at first, then steadily—that his life was bending toward something enormous. Not with sudden force, but with slow, unstoppable intention—like a river choosing its destination long before the traveler ever sees the sea.

In the days that followed, Saul looked at him differently.

Not with anger.

With uncertainty.

Something in David unsettled the king now—not with rebellion, but with gravity. It was as if Saul sensed that the peace David brought did not belong to David alone.

Peace always belongs to something greater.

One evening, after playing for hours to calm another storm in Saul's mind, the king suddenly asked, without looking at him:

"Boy… when you sing, who are you singing to?"

David hesitated.

He had never been asked that.

"Sometimes to Him," he answered carefully. "Sometimes to the dark that tries to swallow Him."

Saul laughed bitterly. "The dark does not swallow gods."

David lifted his eyes slowly.

"No. But it tries to swallow men."

Saul said nothing after that.

But that night, the king dreamed restlessly—and woke with David's words burning behind his eyes.

The court began to whisper.

Some said the shepherd was blessed.

Some said he was dangerous.

Some said he was nothing but a strange boy with strange habits.

Only one thing was certain:

The stars had heard him.

And they do not listen casually.

From then on, David returned to the rooftop often. Sometimes alone. Sometimes after playing until his fingers stiffened and his shoulders ached. Sometimes when confusion grew heavy. Sometimes when joy felt too large to stay trapped inside his chest.

Each time, he sang upward.

Each time, the heavens listened.

And slowly, quietly, invisibly—

A shepherd was being shaped into something the world was not yet ready to name.

CHAPTER IV – The Song of the Hidden Lion: Courage Before Goliath

What David Sang Before He Lifted the Stone

Fear always arrives before giants do.

Long before David ever saw Goliath, he **felt** him.

The battlefield lay in the Valley of Elah, stretching wide and raw between two opposing ridges. On one side stood Israel. On the other, the Philistines. Every morning, as the sun climbed over the hills, the giant emerged. His armor glinted like living fire. His voice rolled across the valley like thunder dragging chains behind it.

And every morning, the army of Israel shrank back.

Goliath did not rush forward. He did not need to. His very presence conquered without moving. He mocked them. He challenged them. He planted terror into their bones with words alone. The soldiers who had once imagined glory now avoided even imagining victory.

David arrived on one of those mornings with bread and grain for his brothers, sent by Jesse who still believed his youngest son belonged only to errands and fields. David was not sent to fight. He was sent to serve.

The moment he entered the camp, he felt the fear.

It was thick. Heavy. Infectious.

Men whispered instead of shouted. They sharpened weapons without meaning to strike. Their eyes scanned the valley, always waiting for the giant to appear again.

David listened.

He did not judge at first. He felt their fear enter him, but it did not take root the way it did in the others. His fear behaved differently. It did not freeze him.

It awakened him.

When Goliath stepped forward again, roaring his challenge into the morning air, David felt the ancient tightening in his chest—the same one he had felt under storm clouds in the fields. The same one he had felt beneath the stars on Saul's rooftop.

Only this time, the darkness had a face.

"Why does no one answer him?" David asked.

His brothers snapped at him.
"Go back to your sheep."
"You do not understand war."
"You are too young."
"You will only die."

David listened.

Then he became very quiet.

He did not answer them with anger. He did not defend himself.

He turned away.

Because something in the giant's voice had stirred something ancient in David—a recognition, not of danger, but of **appointment**.

He did not see a warrior.

He saw a challenge that already belonged to God.

Before David ever picked up a stone, he left the camp alone. He walked to the far edge of the valley where rocks lay scattered along the streambed. The air was tense. The ground trembled faintly under the distant stamping of armored boots.

David knelt beside the water.

And he sang.

Not loudly.
Not defiantly.

Quietly.
Desperately.
Honestly.

"You were with me in the fields.
You were with me in the storm.
If You are not with me now, I will fall.
If You are with me now, nothing stands alone."

His hands moved through the water as he chose five smooth stones—not because he expected to miss, but because his heart still carried the humility of a shepherd.

He stood slowly.

Across the valley, Goliath roared again.

David did not roar back.

He walked forward.

The moment he stepped into the open ground between the armies, everything changed. Thousands of eyes locked onto him at once. The soldiers of Israel froze in horror. The Philistines erupted in laughter.

The giant looked down at him.

"A boy?" Goliath thundered. "They send me a boy?"

David lifted his sling calmly.

"You did not come against me," he answered, his voice steady and clear across the valley, "with sword or spear only. You came with pride. And that has always belonged to my God."

The soldiers trembled.

The sky remained silent.

The giant charged.

And in the instant that followed, something impossible occurred:

David did not feel fear.

He felt **stillness**.

The stillness of the field.
The stillness of the rooftop.
The stillness of the storm answered by song.

The stone flew.

History and breath collided.

And the giant fell.

Israel did not understand what they had witnessed.

They would later say David was brave.
They would later say he was chosen.
They would later say he was unstoppable.

But the truth was simpler—and far more dangerous:

He had already learned how to stand in fear without surrendering to it.

The giant was only the shape fear chose that day.

CHAPTER V – The Blood-Red Psalm: After the Giant Fell

The Soul's Response to Sudden Victory

Victory is louder than defeat.

When Goliath fell, sound exploded across the valley like a broken dam. The Philistine lines buckled in disbelief. The army of Israel surged forward in a roar that had been locked inside their lungs for forty days. Steel clashed. Men shouted. The earth itself seemed to shake under the sudden release of courage that had long been buried under fear.

David stood where the giant had fallen.

He did not cheer.

He did not shout.

He looked at the massive still body before him, the dust settling slowly around it, and for the first time since lifting the sling, he felt his hands begin to tremble.

Not with fear.

With consequence.

The roar of the battlefield felt far away now. The soldiers passed him in waves, charging past to pursue the fleeing Philistines. No one noticed the boy anymore. Not in that moment. The victory had already swallowed him.

David stared at Goliath's face.

Victory had a face now.

And it was terrifying.

He had imagined triumph differently. He had imagined a surge of joy, a feeling of rightness, an immediate peace descending like sunlight after a storm.

Instead, he felt **weight**.

He had taken a life.

Not in rage.
Not in panic.
But in obedience.

That difference disturbed him more than death itself.

He knelt slowly in the dust beside the fallen giant and closed his eyes.

And then, for the first time since the stone left his sling, he sang again.

But this song was different.

This was not the song of courage.

This was the song of aftermath.

"You stood with me when the stone flew.
Stand with me now while the dust settles.
If my hands are Your hands,
teach them how to shake without shame."

The battlefield did not answer.

But his soul listened.

When he finally rose, David was no longer only a shepherd.

And not yet a king.

He walked between two worlds now—the world of innocence behind him and the world of consequence before him. The blood-red dust clung to his sandals as he stepped away from the giant, and he did not wipe it off.

Because this victory had marked him.

He did not yet understand how deeply.

By the time the fighting ended, Israel had crushed the Philistines. The men returned with shouts, spoils, bruises, and glory burning in their eyes. They lifted David onto their shoulders when they saw him again. They shouted his name, laughed, struck his back in celebration.

David let them.

But inside, another battle had begun.

That night, the camp burned with celebration. Fires dotted the valley like fallen stars. Wine flowed freely.

Men spoke loudly of the day, retelling the moment of Goliath's fall again and again, each time larger, louder, more glorious.

David sat slightly apart, the glow of the fire painting his face in gold and shadow.

Someone pressed a drink into his hand.

He did not drink it.

Someone shouted, "Sing for us!"

He did not sing.

Not yet.

Inside him, the blood-red psalm was forming—but it had no words he was ready to speak aloud.

He slipped away from the noise and walked alone to the edge of the valley where the moonlight caught the stones and the fields fell into quiet again. He knelt where the fighting had not reached, where the earth was still untouched by blood.

And there, finally alone, the psalm erupted from him.

"I asked for strength.
You gave me consequence.
I asked for deliverance.
You gave me memory.

If I am to walk further now,
teach me how to carry what I have done."

His voice did not rise in triumph.

It cracked in reverence.

For the first time, David understood something the songs had never taught him before:

Victory does not end the battle.

It only changes its location.

The battlefield had moved from the valley to his heart.

He would carry this battle for the rest of his life.

The next day, when they brought him to Saul in triumph, the king looked at him with eyes that no longer held only relief.

They now held calculation.

Goliath had fallen.

And something even greater had risen.

CHAPTER VI – The Song Saul Was Never Meant to Hear

The Cave Prayer Whispered Under the Threat of Death

Madness does not disappear when it is quieted.

It waits.

For a time, after the giant fell, Saul tried to love David.

At first, he truly did. The boy had saved his kingdom, restored courage to his army, lifted the weight of terror from his throne. Saul kept him close, placed armor upon him, let him ride among warriors who once trembled at the Philistine's roar. The women of Israel sang his name in the streets:

"Saul has slain his thousands,
and David his tens of thousands."

That song was the beginning of the end.

At first, Saul laughed when he heard it.

Then he listened to it.

Then he measured it.

Then he feared it.

And fear, when seated on a throne, does not stay peaceful for long.

David felt the shift before anyone else saw it. It was subtle—an extra second of silence in the room, a glance held too long, a smile that arrived late. The harp still calmed the king, but not fully now. The darkness inside Saul had learned David's sound, and it had grown jealous of it.

One evening, as David played in the royal chamber, the air felt wrong.

Too tense.

Too still.

The candles burned without flickering. Saul sat rigid on his throne, fingers wrapped tightly around his spear. His eyes tracked David's movements—not with relief, but with calculation.

David felt the danger before it moved.

The sound of the harp changed instinctively. He shifted the melody, lowering it, softening it, trying to lead the king away from whatever storm was rising again within him.

It did not work.

Without warning, Saul stood and hurled the spear.

The weapon ripped through the air faster than thought.

David moved without deciding to move. The spear buried itself in the stone wall behind him with a violent crack. For half a heartbeat, they stared at each other in frozen silence—the king with murder in his eyes, the shepherd with death in his shadow.

Then David ran.

From that moment, everything he had known shattered.

The palace became a trap.

The court became hostile ground.

The songs that once healed now made him a target.

Saul did not announce his hatred publicly. He whispered it through shadows. Soldiers began to "coincidentally" appear in David's path at night. Messengers carried him into ambushes disguised as missions. Invitations became tests. Honors became traps.

David learned quickly.

And David fled.

Night after night, he ran through hills, fields, ravines, sleeping where he could, eating what he could find, trusting only a handful of men who slowly gathered around him—warriors who were broken, outcast, in debt, hunted, disillusioned with the king but still loyal to God.

They followed David not because he promised them power.

They followed him because he had no throne to defend.

The caves became their refuge.

Cold. Damp. Dark.

A king without a crown became a leader without walls.

And Saul hunted him.

Relentlessly.

One night, the hunt reached its cruelest moment.

David and his men had taken shelter in a vast cave deep in the wilderness. The entrance was narrow, the interior winding and deep. From the outside, it looked empty.

But inside, hidden in darkness, David and his men lay pressed against the stone, silent as breath held in fear.

Then they heard footsteps.

Torches passed outside.

And then one man entered alone.

King Saul.

He had come to relieve himself, unaware that he had walked directly into the mouth of his enemy's hiding place.

David's men froze.

Their hands tightened on their weapons.

Whispers hissed through the shadows.

"This is the moment."
"God has delivered him into your hands."
"End it."
"Take the throne."

David's heart pounded so loudly he feared Saul might hear it echo in the cave.

The king stood only a few steps away, utterly exposed—his back turned, his guard outside.

A single movement.

One stroke.

One end.

David crept forward slowly, every step silent, every breath measured. His hand shook—not with fear, but with the terrifying realization that he *could* do it.

He lifted his blade.

Saul stirred slightly.

David froze.

And in that frozen instant, something inside him split.

On one side stood destiny.

On the other stood obedience.

David lowered the blade and cut only the edge of Saul's robe.

Then he retreated back into the darkness.

When Saul left the cave, unaware, David's entire body began to tremble violently. He dropped to his knees among his men, shaking as if seized by a fever.

"You spared him," one whispered in disbelief.
"You spared the one who hunts you."

David could barely speak.

"I could not touch what God anointed," he said hoarsely. "Even if God Himself allowed me to reach it."

His men stared at him as at a man both holy and mad.

Then David felt the song rise in him.

Not a song of courage.

Not a song of victory.

A song of terror restrained by faith.

And he sang it **after** Saul had already walked beyond the cave's mouth.

He stepped out into the night air, the torchlight flickering on Saul's retreating form far below, and David cried out—not with rage, not with defiance, but with the raw, broken power of truth:

"My lord the king!" he shouted into the dark.

Saul turned in shock.

David fell on his face before him.

"Why do you listen to voices that say I seek your life?" he cried. "Look! Today I held your death in my hand—and I let you go. Let God judge between us. But my hand will never rise against you."

Saul stood speechless.

The echoes of David's voice faded into the rocks.

And inside his chest, David sang again—this time silently:

"I was hunted.
I was cornered.
I was offered a throne through blood.

And I passed it by.
If I fall now, I fall clean."

Saul wept that night.

But his madness did not die.

The cave had revealed something terrifying to both men:

Saul learned that David would not fall into sin to take the throne.

David learned that obedience would not immediately save his life.

From that night on, David understood the deeper truth:

Righteousness does not prevent suffering.
It only sanctifies it.

And Saul understood something even darker:

He could not destroy David's body without first being judged by David's soul.

The hunt would continue.

But so would the songs.

CHAPTER VII – The Psalm of the Broken Cave: When the Anointed Was Hunted

Faith Forged Under Pursuit

After the cave, David no longer belonged to daylight.

He belonged to shadow and motion.

The wilderness became his kingdom—dry ravines, jagged highlands, cracked earth scorched by the sun and frozen by the night. The places where no banners flew. The places where songs had to be whispered so they did not betray life itself.

Saul did not stop hunting.

If anything, the cave made the pursuit more savage.

The king no longer chased David as a rival.

He chased him as a threat ordained by God.

And when a ruler believes heaven itself has turned against him, he becomes more dangerous than any enemy army.

David moved constantly.

One night in the hills.
Another in abandoned ruins.
Another among strangers who feared him but offered bread quietly when they saw the scars on his men.

His following grew—but not with heroes.

The broken came to him.

Men drowned in debt.
Men haunted by defeat.
Men rejected by their own clans.
Men who had nothing left to lose but their shame.

They arrived in silence.

And David received them without questions.

He did not recruit an army.

He gathered refugees of life.

At first, their fear was thick. They flinched at every sound. They argued, doubted, panicked. Some begged David to fight back openly. Some begged him to flee forever into foreign lands.

David listened.

And then he led them deeper into the wilderness.

Not to hide.

To be stripped.

The caves became their shelter.

Dark, breathing stone.

Dripping walls.

Air thin and cold.

Here, David's faith was no longer poetic.

It was survival.

One night, Saul's forces came so close that the men could hear armor scraping rock outside the cave mouth. Torches flickered on the walls. The breath of the soldiers disturbed the stale air.

Some of David's men shook openly.

One whispered, "This is the end."

Another said, "If we rush them, maybe one of us escapes."

David did not answer.

He stood with his back against the cold stone and felt something crack silently inside his chest.

Not fear.

Trust.

He realized then that his faith had changed again.

In the fields, he had trusted God for safety.
Before Goliath, he had trusted God for victory.
Before Saul in the cave, he had trusted God for restraint.

Now… he had to trust God for **presence without outcome**.

For the first time, David sang without knowing if he would live through the psalm.

His voice was barely more than breath.

"You placed me in darkness,
but You did not abandon me to it.
If I die here, I die facing You.
If I live, I live by Your breath alone."

Outside, the soldiers eventually moved on.

But inside the cave, David fell to his knees and wept silently until his ribs ached.

Not because he was afraid of dying.

Because he was exhausted from becoming unkillable through obedience.

The men began to change.

At first they followed him out of desperation.

Then they followed him out of conviction.

They stopped demanding answers.

They stopped measuring success by victory.

They learned to listen the way David listened—to silence, to fear, to God.

And David began to understand what kind of leader he truly was becoming:

Not a conqueror.

A furnace.

And anyone who stayed would be forged by suffering and faith together.

One evening, after weeks of flight, they rested in a shattered cave so broken that moonlight poured through the collapsed ceiling like silver dust. The men slept in uneven circles, weapons close, bodies thin, spirits stretched.

David remained awake.

He always did.

It was in that broken cave that the next psalm was born—not from threat, not from terror, but from **weariness**.

The kind of weariness that does not scream…

It whispers.

"How long must the hunted become holy
before the throne is allowed to exist?
How long must promise feel like mockery
before it becomes truth?"

His voice trembled.

"You anointed me with oil.
Now You anoint me with dust.
If this is the weight of the crown,
teach me how to carry it without breaking."

And something within the cave shifted.

Not the stone.

The men.

One by one, they woke—not to sound, but to atmosphere. The broken discovered that the darkness no longer felt hostile.

It felt sacred.

From that night forward, the cave was no longer only refuge.

It was a **sanctuary of transformation**.

But Saul did not slow.

The king's wrath began to consume everything around it.

He slaughtered priests who had helped David unknowingly.

He punished villages suspected of loyalty to the shepherd.

His kingdom began to rot under the weight of obsession.

And David knew it.

He felt it in prayer like distant thunder approaching.

He began to understand something terrifying:

His obedience was destroying Saul…

without him lifting a single weapon.

One night, Jonathan—Saul's son—found David secretly. The two met beneath a grove of trees, neither knowing if they would ever see the other again.

"My father will never stop," Jonathan said quietly. "He is no longer fighting you. He is fighting God."

David lowered his eyes.

"I do not want to be king this way," he said. "Not through madness."

Jonathan placed his hand on David's shoulder.

"Kingship does not ask permission. It reveals itself through what you refuse to do."

That night, David sang alone again.

Not for Saul.

Not for the men.

For himself.

"If the crown comes through blood,
may it die on my head before it lives in my hand.
If the throne comes through obedience,
may I never outrun the wilderness that taught me."

Days later, Saul's army surrounded another cave.

Arrows flew.

Men fell.

David escaped by fracture of timing so precise it felt impossible.

When the dust settled, his followers realized it again:

They were still alive.

Because their leader would not kill to survive.

And that realization changed them permanently.

They no longer followed David because he would protect them.

They followed him because he would not become Saul to do so.

And that is a far rarer kind of leader.

That night, David looked at his scarred hands by firelight and understood something that would shape every decision for the rest of his life:

The throne was not delayed.
It was being purified through pressure.

The cave did not break him.

It broke the part of him that could have ruled without trembling.

And that made all the difference.

CHAPTER VIII – The Song of the Loyal Warrior: Jonathan's Secret Covenant

The Friendship That Bound Two Destinies

Some friendships are born in laughter.

Others are born in survival.

But the rarest friendships are born in **sacrifice**—when two destinies recognize one another and choose unity over rivalry.

This was the friendship of David and Jonathan.

It began the day David returned from the valley with the dust of Goliath still clinging to his skin. Saul watched him with suspicion. The court watched him with awe. But Jonathan—Saul's son, heir to the throne—watched him with recognition.

Not recognition of strength alone.

Recognition of spirit.

Jonathan had been raised for power from the day he could stand. Armor had been placed on his shoulders before he ever learned fear. Strategy had shaped his thinking before he learned mercy. He was brave, disciplined, respected—but inside him lived a quiet loneliness.

Because he had always known he was expected to be king.

And destiny, when imposed too early, can feel like a prison even when it is wrapped in gold.

So when Jonathan saw David walk back into camp without armor, without boasting, without even lifting his head to receive praise—something inside him shifted.

The shepherd had what the prince had never been allowed to develop:

freedom of the soul.

That very evening, Jonathan sought him out.

They met in a quiet corridor beyond the noise of celebration. David was washing dust and dried blood from his hands. Jonathan stood in silence for several moments before speaking.

"You are not afraid of death," Jonathan said.

David glanced at him and shrugged. "I am afraid of many things. I simply chose not to let fear choose for me today."

Jonathan smiled faintly at that.

And in that moment, something deeper than words passed between them.

They talked long into the night—about battle, about God, about fear, about the wilderness, about what it means to obey something unseen when everything visible demands otherwise.

By morning, they were no longer strangers.

They were bound.

Not by ambition.
Not by blood.
But by **alignment**.

As David's fame grew and Saul's jealousy hardened, Jonathan found himself trapped between two worlds—his father's throne and his friend's destiny.

And that is where loyalty becomes costly.

The first time Jonathan warned David that Saul intended to kill him, it nearly broke him to speak the words aloud.

"My father is not thinking clearly," Jonathan said, his voice tight. "He fears you more than he fears the Philistines now."

David lowered his eyes, pain flickering across his face. "I never sought his throne."

Jonathan nodded slowly. "That is exactly why he fears you."

From that moment on, Jonathan became David's shield inside the palace. He spoke to Saul in David's defense. He delayed assassinations with excuses. He redirected soldiers. He sent coded messages through servants who knew how to keep their mouths shut.

Each act of protection placed him one step closer to betrayal in the eyes of his own father.

Yet he did not stop.

Because Jonathan had seen something Saul could no longer see:

David's rise was not rebellion. It was revelation.

One night, when Saul's pursuit sharpened beyond concealment, Jonathan and David met secretly in a field beyond the city. They spoke in whispers beneath olive trees that leaned like silent witnesses over their fate.

"My father will stop at nothing," Jonathan said. "Tomorrow you must flee."

David's chest tightened. "And you?"

Jonathan's voice did not waver. "I remain."

David stepped back as if struck. "You will be standing on the wrong side of history."

Jonathan shook his head. "No. I will be standing on the right side of obedience."

Then Jonathan did something that stunned David completely.

He removed his royal robe—the symbol of his inheritance, the visible promise that one day the throne of Israel would belong to him—and placed it around David's shoulders.

Then his armor.

Then his sword.

Then his belt.

Each piece passed from prince to shepherd with quiet finality.

Jonathan knelt.

"God has chosen you," he said. "And I will not fight God to preserve my pride."

David's breath caught painfully in his chest. He had faced giants without trembling—but this humility shattered him.

"You need not bow to me," David whispered.

"I bow to the will of the Eternal," Jonathan replied. "You just happen to be standing in its shadow."

They clasped forearms as brothers.

And there in the field, beneath the quiet watching of heaven, they made the **secret covenant**:

That neither ambition nor throne nor blood would turn them into enemies.
That loyalty would not bend before power.
That even if destiny tore them apart in position, it would never divide them in spirit.

Jonathan would protect David as long as breath remained in him.

David would never raise his hand against Saul for Jonathan's sake.

They sealed it with tears.

Not the tears of fear.

The tears of knowing that obedience sometimes demands the surrender of everything visible.

When David fled into the wilderness for the final time, Jonathan watched from the ridge of the city until the night swallowed his silhouette completely.

That night, David sang a new psalm—not of refuge, not of pursuit, but of **friendship forged in destiny**:

"You gave me a brother without sharing blood.
You gave me loyalty without demanding crowns.
If I wear a throne one day,
let it never erase the kneeling prince who placed it there."

Jonathan would never sit on that throne.

He would die before it was ever David's.

But his loyalty would live inside David longer than Saul's hatred ever could.

Because not all warriors fight with swords.

Some fight with surrender.

And those battles echo beyond death.

CHAPTER IX – The Wilderness Lament: Forty Nights Without a Throne

How the Desert Shaped the Future King

The wilderness does not announce itself.

It does not thunder like armies.
It does not roar like giants.
It does not whisper like betrayal.

It simply *waits*.

And when a man enters it carrying destiny on his back and fear in his chest, the wilderness takes everything that is false—and leaves only what can survive without applause.

David entered the desert as a fugitive.

Not as a king.

Not as a conqueror.

Not even as a hero.

He entered as a man hunted by the army he once served, betrayed by the throne he once calmed with music, abandoned by the safety he never truly possessed.

And the desert received him without pity.

The first ten nights were brutality.

Thirst scorched his throat until his tongue felt like cracked leather. Food was scarce. Bread grew stale after one day. Meat became a memory. Sleep came in broken fragments, interrupted by distant hoofbeats, imagined footsteps, sudden panic that the firelight would give him away.

His men suffered quietly.

Some cursed Saul.
Some cursed the desert.
Some cursed God.

David said nothing.

He led them deeper.

Not toward safety.

Toward stripping.

By the twentieth night, something inside the group began to fracture. Strong men who once demanded commands now sat with hollow eyes. Arguments turned petty. Faith grew thin. One night, two men fought over a waterskin so violently that David had to separate them himself.

That night, alone beneath a frozen sky, David sang again—not loudly, not with confidence, but with **grief**:

"You promised oil on my head.
You promised presence in my steps.
But You did not promise bread in my hands.
Teach me how to trust You hungry."

And the desert answered in the only way it ever does:

By staying silent.

By the thirtieth night, his men were no longer soldiers or warriors.

They were **students of survival**.

Every movement was measured. Every sound was controlled. Every resource was shared. Pride vanished. Status vanished. Titles vanished. Even fear began to change shape—not disappear, but refine.

David noticed it in their eyes.

These men were no longer surviving because he was strong.

They were surviving because **they trusted**.

And trust is more rare than courage.

On the thirty-fourth night, Saul's scouts passed so close to their hiding place that David could hear a soldier muttering to himself. A single mistake would have ended everything. One cough. One shifted stone. One careless spark.

David pressed his men into the ground, his hand raised in silence. Forty breaths passed like forty years.

No one moved.

Not even in panic.

When the danger passed, no one celebrated.

They simply remained still.

And in that stillness, David understood something terrifying and holy:

These men would follow him to death—not because he promised victory, but because he had learned how to wait with them.

On the fortieth night, David could no longer ignore the ache within him.

Forty nights without a throne.
Forty nights without promise made visible.

Forty nights without evidence that the anointing had not been a mistake.

The men slept.

David walked alone into the open desert.

The sky stretched endless and merciless above him. The stars felt distant now—not intimate like before, but silent like judges who refuse to speak.

And for the first time since his youth, David **lamented** without softness.

"How long will I be called what I am not allowed to become?" he cried.
"How long must I survive before I live?"
"How long must obedience feel like punishment?"

His knees collapsed into the sand.

"I did not take Saul's life.
I did not take the throne by force.
If this is the cost of being clean—
tell me, God, if it is worth paying forever."

His voice cracked in anger and exhaustion.

And into that raw question, something quiet entered him—not a promise, not a vision, not a miracle.

Understanding.

David saw it then:

The desert was not delaying the throne.

It was **teaching him how not to become Saul when he finally reached it.**

Saul had received power before he learned obedience.

David was learning obedience before he ever touched power.

That was the difference between a ruler who panics and a ruler who endures.

David rose slowly.

The desert had not answered him with words—but it had answered him with shaping.

The next morning, the men noticed something different in him.

Not confidence.

Not ferocity.

Weight.

He carried himself differently.

Not like a man waiting for destiny.

Like a man prepared to survive it.

From that day forward, David no longer spoke of the throne.

He spoke of:

Responsibility.
Restraint.
Unity.
Listening.

He trained them not only to fight—but to govern themselves.

He settled disputes without favoritism.
He divided food with fairness.
He punished with reluctance, not rage.
He rewarded without creating envy.

Unseen, unnoticed by nations, a **kingdom was being built inside a cave-strewn wilderness.**

And the world had no idea.

At the end of the fortieth night, David sang again—but not a desperate song.

This was steadier.

"This desert did not kill me.
It slaughtered the king I was tempted to become.

If I ever sit on a throne,
let these nights sit with me forever."

The men did not hear him.

But the future did.

The wilderness had completed its first great work.

It had removed David's hunger for power.

And in doing so, it prepared him to receive it without poison.

CHAPTER X – The Song of the Crown Laid Down in Tears

What David Felt When He Finally Became King

The throne did not arrive with thunder.

It came with news carried by trembling lips.

Saul was dead.

Jonathan was dead.

The battlefield on Mount Gilboa had swallowed both king and prince in one single, catastrophic night. The crown of Israel lay in blood-soaked dust, and the future had arrived not as celebration, but as shock.

David heard the words in a wilderness stronghold far from the palace he had fled years before. A messenger came running, torn clothes clinging to his body, face hollow with terror and exhaustion.

"The king is fallen," the man gasped.
"And Jonathan… Jonathan is with him."

For a moment, David did not move.

Not because he did not understand.

But because the weight of the words was too complete to land all at once.

Then it broke him.

He did not shout.

He did not rage.

He did not seize the air in triumph.

He collapsed.

His knees struck the floor hard enough to bruise. His hands shook violently as if the desert cold had returned to claim his bones.

Jonathan was gone.

The wilderness had prepared him for hunger, for pursuit, for fear, for delay—but it had not prepared him for this.

David tore his garment and fell with his face to the earth. His men stood frozen around him, warriors hardened by pursuit and survival, yet powerless in the face of their leader's grief.

That night, David sang the most devastating song of his life.

Not to request mercy.

Not to ask guidance.

But to mourn what destiny had demanded in advance.

"Your love was greater to me than crowns.
Your loyalty guarded me when stone and spear failed.
How does a throne breathe when the friend who gave it is buried beneath it?"

The men listened in silence.

There was no victory in his voice.

Only burial.

The kingdom waited.

But David remained on his knees.

The Crown That Did Not Feel Like Reward

It took time before Judah came to him.

Not immediately.

Not eagerly.

Power always hesitates when it no longer knows who commands it.

Elders arrived one by one. They spoke carefully. They measured him with cautious eyes. And finally, they offered him the crown of Judah.

David did not stand immediately.

He did not rush forward.

Instead, he asked one question:

"Where are the sons of Saul?"

The elders shifted uncomfortably.

"They are scattered," one answered. "The throne is yours now."

David closed his eyes.

"Then I do not take it as trophy," he said. "I take it as mourning."

When they poured the oil upon his head, he wept openly.

Not like a conqueror.

But like a man burying what might have been.

The people expected a roar.

They received a sob.

The crown touched his head—and he trembled.

Because oil may make a king.

But it does not heal a heart.

The Weight of a Throne No One Else Could Feel

That first night as king, David did not sleep in a palace.

He slept on the floor.

The crown lay beside him.

He stared at it in the dark.

For years he had been hunted for it.

Now that it rested within his reach, it felt unbearably heavy.

He whispered into the silence:

"I did not run from Saul to sit where he sat.
I ran so I would not become who he became."

His breath shook.

"If this throne demands what the last one did,
break it before it breaks me."

No voice answered.

But something inside him steadied.

The Long War That Followed the Crown

David's coronation did not bring peace.

It brought war.

The house of Saul fought for years to hold what blood had already surrendered. Brothers rose against brothers. Tribes divided. Assassins prowled like shadows. Trust came slowly and bled easily.

David fought—but differently than Saul had.

He did not chase revenge.

He waited for alignment.

He did not kill recklessly.

He judged reluctantly.

He listened to the weak.

He fed the wounded.

He buried enemies with honor.

And everywhere he went, people noticed something unsettling:

This king fought...
but he was not fueled by thirst.

He was fueled by **responsibility**.

The Day All Israel Came

Years passed.

Then one day, the elders of all Israel came to Hebron.

They stood before him not with weapons.

With surrender.

"You were the true shepherd of this nation even when Saul sat on the throne," they said. "You guarded us in your wilderness. Now lead us in the open."

This time, the oil was poured without hesitation.

This time, the people sang.

And David... cried again.

Because the crown he now received had been baptized in:

- Flight
- Starvation
- Betrayal
- Fidelity
- Death
- Friendship
- Restraint

It was not a prize.

It was a **consequence**.

The Song That No One Heard in the Palace

That night, once alone, David did not sing loudly.

He whispered the final tear-song of becoming:

"You chased me into darkness
so I could carry light without burning.
You made me small

so I would not crush what I rule.
If I ever forget these tears,
take the throne from me before You take my soul."

And that was the true coronation.

Not the trumpet.

Not the oil.

Not the crowd.

But the moment a shepherd promised God he would never forget the dust on his knees.

CHAPTER XI – The Psalm of the Dancing King

Sacred Ecstasy Before the Ark

Power teaches a man how to stand.

But only God teaches a king how to fall to his knees without shame.

David had conquered Jerusalem by strategy and courage. The city had resisted kings for centuries, fortified by stone and pride. Now it belonged to Israel. And with it came the longing that had burned in David's chest from the first days of his anointing:

To bring the Ark of God home.

The Ark was not a symbol to him.

It was memory.

It was presence.

It was terror and intimacy bound together in gold and wood.

For years it had rested in obscurity, distant from the center of leadership, treated like a dangerous relic rather than the living heartbeat of the nation. David could not rule while God remained on the margins.

So he gathered the people.

Not an army.

A procession.

Singers.
Drummers.
Priests trembling beneath sacred weight.
Common men who had never seen the Ark but felt something older than memory pulling at their bones.

When the Ark was lifted onto the cart, the air thickened.

Not with fear.

With expectation.

David wore not royal robes that day.

He wore linen.

The garment of servants.

The garment of priests.

The garment of men who had nothing to protect but obedience.

The procession began slowly.

Every step felt deliberate.

The oxen strained.

The people held their breath.

Then the unthinkable happened.

One of the men guiding the Ark stumbled. Instinctively, he reached out to steady it. The moment his hand touched the sacred chest, his body collapsed.

Dead.

Instant.

No cry.

No warning.

The celebration shattered into horror.

The music stopped.

The drums fell silent.

The singers froze in terror.

And David—David backed away as if struck by lightning.

The same presence that healed with songs could also kill with holiness.

God was not tame.

The Ark was left where it stood.

The people scattered in fear.

And David went home shaken to his core.

That night, he did not sing.

That night, he wrestled with dread.

"Why must Your nearness be so frightening?" he whispered into darkness.
"Why does the same presence that delivers also destroy?"

For three months, the Ark remained in another house—and blessings poured out over that household. Crops flourished. Children were healed. Fields overflowed.

David watched from a distance.

And slowly, his fear gave way to understanding:

Holiness is not the enemy.

Presumption is.

When the second procession was prepared, everything was different.

This time, the Ark was lifted not by carts—but by shoulders.
This time, there were pauses every six steps.
This time, blood was offered in reverence.
This time, no one treated the presence of God casually.

And this time...

David did not walk.

He exploded into movement.

The moment the first step was taken safely, something ancient tore free inside him. The king who had learned restraint in caves now learned abandon in light.

He danced.

Not as a performer.

Not as a politician.

Not as a ruler.

As a man *incapable of containing gratitude*.

His feet struck the earth with rhythm that did not come from drums.

His arms lifted without calculation.

He spun.

He leapt.

He laughed aloud with tears streaming openly.

The nation stared.

The soldiers blinked in shock.

The elders shifted uncomfortably.

And from the palace window, Michal—Saul's daughter, David's wife—watched in frozen disbelief.

This was not how kings behaved.

There was no dignity here.

No controlled posture.

No political precision.

Only ecstasy.

Only surrender.

Only a heart exploding in the presence of the One it had sung to since boyhood.

David did not see the window.

He saw only the Ark.

And the God who walked once among sheep and storms and valleys now walked again through the city of kings.

When the Ark was finally set in its place and the feast prepared, David returned toward the palace still burning with light.

Michal confronted him at the doors.

"How glorious the king of Israel looked today," she said coldly. "Uncovering himself like a common fool before servant girls."

The music inside David stopped.

He looked at her—not with anger, not with pride, but with aching clarity.

"It was before the Lord," he said quietly.
"The One who chose me above your father and his house."

She scoffed.

David continued, his voice steady:

"I will become even more undignified than this.
I will be humiliated in my own eyes—
just to remain near Him."

Michal turned away in disgust.

David turned back toward the Ark.

And in that instant, their lives separated permanently—
not by divorce, but by devotion.

She remained queen by title.

He remained king by surrender.

That night, while the city feasted, David once again sang alone.

Not in sorrow.

In blazing joy.

"You took me from sheep
and did not erase the field from my soul.
You gave me a crown
and I danced it back to You.
If the world is offended by my joy,
let it be—
for my soul remembers who carried it first."

This was the psalm of the dancing king.

Not written.

Not recorded.

But lived so loudly that even generations later, people would still wonder:

What kind of ruler dares to lose himself in God without fear of losing his power?

And the answer was simple:

A ruler who learned God before he ever learned applause.

CHAPTER XII – The Song of Silent Guilt: Before Bathsheba Was Seen

When Temptation Approached Unseen

Temptation does not begin with desire.

It begins with **fatigue**.

After years of battle, flight, waiting, hunger, pursuit, coronation, and war for unity, David finally stood secure on his throne. The surrounding nations had been subdued. Jerusalem was fortified. The Ark rested near the center of his rule. His name now carried weight far beyond Israel's borders.

And for the first time since his youth, **nothing was chasing him anymore**.

No Saul.
No exile.
No caves.
No constant urgency.
No visible enemy.

That was when danger truly arrived.

Not as war.

As quiet.

The season came when kings usually rode out at the head of their armies. The roads filled with dust and armor. Trumpets signaled campaigns. Men proved loyalty with blood and scars.

But David stayed home.

No single decision doomed him that year. There was no thunderclap of rebellion inside his heart. No dramatic fall. No open betrayal of conscience.

There was only a slow loosening of vigilance.

A subtle shift.

A man who had lived on the edge of death began to taste comfort.

Late mornings replaced early marches. Soft garments replaced leather and steel. Meals came without ration. Wine flowed without counting. The body that had once endured hunger now learned abundance.

And the soul, if not guarded, grows careless in abundance.

David still prayed.

But his prayers grew shorter.

David still sang.

But his songs no longer rose from desperation.

He still ruled with wisdom—but now without trembling.

And the trembling, though painful, had once protected him.

One evening, as the sun slid down behind the western hills, David walked alone onto the roof of his palace. From there, Jerusalem spread beneath him in layered rooftops, courtyards, shadows, cooking fires, laughter drifting faintly through the air.

The city was at peace.

And peace can be more dangerous than war.

David leaned against the parapet and let his thoughts drift. He was not thinking about sin. Not about desire. Not about betrayal. He was simply **idle**.

An idle heart is never empty.

It simply begins to fill with what it once outran.

He began to think of his youth.
Of the fields.
Of loneliness.
Of the hunger he no longer felt.
Of the isolation power had brought him even as it crowned him.

For a moment, bitterness flickered through him.

"I gave everything," he thought. "And still I stand alone."

He pushed the thought away.

But it returned.

Not as complaint.

As permission.

That was the first crack.

David did not yet see Bathsheba.
But the **song of silent guilt had already begun**.

The guards no longer questioned his wanderings at night. The palace servants had learned when not to look up. Orders flowed smoothly. The machinery of power functioned without resistance.

And slowly, invisibly, David began to forget what it had cost him to reach this place.

He remembered Saul's madness—but not the terror of the spear.
He remembered the cave—but not the shaking in the dark.
He remembered the crown—but not the tears when it touched his head.

Memory softened.

And softened memory is fertile soil for illusion.

One night, lying sleepless beneath fine linens, David felt the old restlessness return. But this time it was not spiritual hunger. It was not longing for God.

It was longing for **something unnamed**.

He rose and walked the corridors again. The lamps burned low. The palace breathed quietly. His footsteps echoed faintly in empty halls lined with trophies of victory.

And still he felt hollow.

He stepped onto the rooftop again.

The city stirred far below.

Windows glowed.

Shadows moved.

Life, intimate and private, unfolded beneath the king who could command anything—but not the quiet ache inside his chest.

And for the first time in years, David did not sing.

He simply watched.

This was the moment temptation approaches unseen.

Not with heat.

With silence.

Not with urgency.

With wandering.

Not with hunger.

With entitlement disguised as loneliness.

David had not yet sinned.

But he was drifting toward the edge of **self-justification**.

"I have earned rest."
"I have earned comfort."
"I have earned a moment for myself."

Those words had never lived in him before.

Now they began to whisper.

The next days passed normally. Councils were held. Judgments were rendered. Gifts arrived from foreign lands. Messengers brought news of victory from distant battlefields.

David nodded.

Blessed.

Honored.

Secure.

And subtly... detached.

He no longer asked the question that once guided every decision:

"What will this require of my obedience?"

Now he began asking:

"What will this cost me personally?"

The shift was tiny.

But fatal.

Then came the night.

The air was warm. The city slept beneath clear skies. David walked once more onto the rooftop—not seeking anything in particular.

And that is when he saw her.

But the true tragedy of that moment is not that he saw Bathsheba.

It is that **he had already given himself permission to look**.

The silent guilt had prepared the ground.

What happened next would shatter kings, families, bloodlines, and legacy.

But the fall did not begin with her.

It began here.

With a king at rest who forgot why he had once trembled.

With a heart no longer desperate for God.

With a man who had survived war—but had not prepared for ease.

And somewhere in the deep chambers of his soul, the song he no longer sang returned—distorted now, no longer protective.

The song of silent guilt.

CHAPTER XIII – The Psalm Born from Adultery and Fire

The Cry of Shame and the Hunger for Forgiveness

The night David saw Bathsheba did not feel like a fall.

It felt like a pause.

A pause in which he believed—falsely—that the rules of consequence had stopped applying to him.

She moved within the quiet privacy of her courtyard, unaware of the eyes above. The water caught the moonlight. The moment seemed ordinary. Human. Brief.

David turned away at first.

That first turn could have ended everything.

But temptation never demands immediately.

It invites.

He turned back.

And with that return of the eyes, a far greater return began inside him—the return of a hunger he had not felt since youth, but without the discipline that once guarded it.

He sent for information.

Not out of lust at first, but out of **curiosity**—the deadliest form of permission.

"She is Bathsheba," the servant said carefully. "The wife of Uriah the Hittite. One of your own mighty men."

The warning was clear.

The boundary was visible.

David heard it.

And did not retreat.

Power had quietly taught him that barriers were **negotiable**.

He sent for her.

What happened between them was not a moment of romance.

It was a collision between authority and vulnerability, between loneliness and opportunity, between a king who had stopped trembling and a woman who had no real power to refuse.

It was fast.

And it was final.

When she left the palace that night, David stood alone again—but something inside him had fractured.

Weeks passed.

The war continued far from Jerusalem.

Then the message came.

"I am with child."

David stared at the words as if they were written in fire.

Now the sin demanded **architecture**.

Covering shame requires more creativity than committing it.

At first, David attempted mercy.

He called Uriah home from battle and urged him to return to his wife. Uriah refused—out of loyalty to the army, to the ark, to the men sleeping in open fields. His obedience mocked David's betrayal.

David tried again.

Wine this time.

Still Uriah would not go.

And in that refusal, David faced the truth:

He could not fix this with kindness.

So he chose calculation.

A sealed letter was sent to the battlefield.

Uriah carried his own death order without knowing it.

"Place him where the fighting is fiercest. Then withdraw."

Uriah died as instructed.

And the world called it war.

Bathsheba mourned.

Then was taken into the palace.

The child would appear legitimate.

The secret would survive.

David had built a shelter for his sin.

But inside, there was no shelter at all.

For the first time since the caves, David did not sing.

Weeks turned into months.

He ruled normally.

Judged wisely.

Led strategically.

But something within him decayed in silence.

Not loudly.

Internally.

Every victory rang hollow.

Every song tasted bitter.

Every prayer stopped just short of heaven.

And now the sweetness of comfort had turned into the stench of rot that only a guilty king can smell in his own soul.

Then Nathan came.

The prophet did not accuse him directly.

He told him a story.

A rich man.

A poor man.

A single lamb stolen.

David's rage ignited instantly.

"That man deserves death!"

Nathan stepped forward.

And spoke the words that shattered a throne:

"You are the man."

The impact was nuclear.

All architecture collapsed.

All justification evaporated.

All strategy turned to ash.

David did not argue.

He did not deny.

He did not defend.

He did not explain.

He **collapsed inward**.

"I have sinned against the Lord."

Nathan's voice was steady:

"The Lord has taken away your sin. But the sword will never depart from your house."

Forgiveness came.

Consequence remained.

The child fell ill.

David fasted.

Prayed.

Wept.

Refused food.

Lay on the floor like a man trying to bend death with grief.

The servants whispered that he had lost his mind.

Seven days passed.

On the seventh... the child died.

The servants were afraid to tell him.

When he realized the silence had changed, he rose slowly from the ground.

He washed.

He ate.

And the servants were stunned.

"You fasted while the child lived," they asked. "Why eat now?"

David answered with eyes hollow but clear:

"I fasted in hope.
Now I accept in truth."

That day, David sang again.

Not from triumph.

Not from strength.

But from **ruin**.

The psalm born from adultery and fire was not beautiful.

It was honest.

He did not ask to escape consequence.

He asked only not to be abandoned **inside** consequence.

He would never escape what he had set in motion.

His household would fracture.

His sons would turn on him.

Blood would answer blood.

And every wound would trace its origin to this one night.

But forgiveness had begun.

Not the removal of scars.

The cleansing of the soul beneath them.

David would never again judge another man's sin lightly.

And he would never again assume that falling meant God had left.

But he would also never again believe that power was safe.

The fire had touched him at last.

And he had learned what all kings eventually learn:

Victory over enemies is loud.

Victory over self is silent.

And falls always echo longer than triumphs.

CHAPTER XIV – The Song of the Prophet's Finger: When Nathan Spoke

The Word That Shattered the King

David thought the worst moment had already passed.

He believed the breaking had ended with the death of the child.

He believed that once the fast was over, once the body was washed, once food touched his lips again, the deepest collapse had already happened.

He was wrong.

The collapse of the body is loud.

The collapse of the **identity** comes later.

Days after the child was buried, David returned to the routines of rule. He sat again in the hall of judgment. He issued commands. He listened to disputes. He received reports from the battlefield. His voice was steady. His posture was firm. To the watching eyes of the court, the king appeared restored.

But inside him, something critical had detached.

He felt as though he were ruling from behind glass.

He understood every word spoken to him, yet none of it touched his center. Applause meant nothing. Displeasure meant nothing. He was present—but hollowed.

And it was in that condition that Nathan came again.

Not as a storyteller this time.

Not as a mirror.

But as a messenger of final alignment.

The prophet entered the court without announcement. He did not bow deeply. He did not flatter. His eyes met David's directly, without caution.

David felt the shift immediately.

This was not another parable.

This was reckoning without metaphor.

"David," Nathan said calmly, "the Lord has spoken again."

The room grew quiet.

The servants stepped back.

The air itself felt like it had tightened.

David nodded once. "Speak."

Nathan did not raise his voice.

That made it worse.

"You have been forgiven," the prophet said. "But forgiveness does not erase structure. What has been set in motion will now mature."

David's jaw tightened.

"This house," Nathan continued, "will divide. What you buried in secret will rise in daylight. What you took in silence will be taken from you in the open. The sword you sent by letter will not leave your roof."

The words did not wound like accusation.

They **settled** like architecture.

David did not interrupt.

He could feel the truth assembling around him like walls closing into place.

"Your sons will rise against one another," Nathan said. "Your authority will be mocked from within your bloodline."
"The danger you once fled from the outside will now be born inside your house."

The king finally spoke, his voice low and strained.

"Is there no stopping this?"

Nathan's eyes softened—but did not retreat.

"There is no cancellation," he said. "Only navigation."

David closed his eyes slowly.

The throne beneath him felt suddenly meaningless.

"So this is what forgiveness looks like," he whispered.

Nathan answered gently:

"This is what **alignment after fracture** looks like."

The prophet turned and left.

But David did not move.

The hammer had already fallen.

And now the structure of consequence would rise slowly around him, year by year, son by son, betrayal by betrayal.

The Kingdom That Continued While the Soul Limped

David ruled well.

That was the terror of it.

The nation prospered.

Trade flourished.

Borders held.

Enemies remained at bay.

The priests sang.

The people rejoiced.

And the king sat among them as a man with a healed reputation and a wounded core.

He no longer led with innocence.

He led with memory.

Every judgment he rendered passed through his own crime first. Every accusation echoed with his own guilt before it ever found another's ear. He no longer viewed sin as distant from power—but as something that sleeps inside it.

He governed with restraint.

But restraint does not erase regret.

The palace grew fuller.

Children grew.

Rivalries formed.

Whispers traveled servants' corridors.

David watched them with a fearful awareness he had never possessed before.

He now knew that **the battle he feared most would not come from armies**.

It would rise from sons.

The Silent Psalm That Followed Judgment

One night, long after the court had slept, David returned to the same rooftop where temptation had once found him wandering.

Jerusalem lay quiet beneath him.

The same city.

The same stones.

The same stars.

But not the same man.

He did not sing aloud.

He did not move at first.

He simply stood and let the weight of the prophet's words crush fully into his awareness.

"You buried the sin," he whispered. "I uncovered the future."

His hands trembled—not with lust now, but with the realization that forgiveness does not undo pathways already chosen.

And then, slowly, the second layer of this season descended upon him:

Not shame.

Responsibility.

He realized then that he was no longer living for his own soul alone.

He was living as the root from which many branches would grow—and some of those branches would twist, break, and wound others.

And he would still be blamed.

And rightly so.

David understood then why God had not removed the consequences.

Because consequences teach the nation what mercy alone cannot.

That night, the song inside him took a terrible, quiet form:

"I will not ask to escape what I set in motion.
But I will ask for strength not to abandon those who bleed from it.
If my house must suffer,
let it not suffer without a king who remains present."

This psalm was never sung in the Temple.

It was too heavy for choirs.

The King Who Would Now Rule While Awaiting the Storm

From that moment on, David lived with two visions in his mind at all times:

The kingdom as it was.

And the kingdom as it would be torn.

He saw laughter—but he also saw knives.

He heard children play—but he also heard echoes of war in their voices.

Every smile in his household carried shadow now.

And yet—he did not withdraw.

He loved harder.

He taught deeper.

He listened more slowly.

He hesitated where once he commanded.

His leadership matured into something heavier than authority:

Endurance.

He knew a storm was coming.

But he would not hide from it.

Why This Song Shattered Him More Than the Accusation

Nathan's first words had crushed David's pride.

Nathan's second words crushed his illusion that repentance ends all fire.

David learned that day what many never understand:

Repentance does not rewind time.

It **reorients the future inside the wreckage of the past**.

From that day forward, David no longer feared exposure.

He feared impact.

Not what would be revealed about him—

But what would be unleashed through him.

CHAPTER XV – The Psalm of Ashes and Repentance

The Road Back from Spiritual Ruin

Repentance does not begin when a man admits he is wrong.

It begins when he realizes he is **broken**.

David had confessed.
He had fasted.
He had lost the child.
He had received Nathan's judgment.

But these moments, as devastating as they were, were only the surface.
True repentance is not an event—it is a descent.

And David had not yet reached the bottom.

The Days When Silence Became His Judge

In the weeks that followed Nathan's visitation, David found himself avoiding mirrors—not polished bronze, not water, not even the eyes of servants. When others looked at him, he felt a quiet accusation even if none was spoken.

He had always been a king who listened to the suffering of his people.
Now he felt he carried their suffering in his own veins.

He spoke less.

He prayed more.

But his prayers did not rise.

They fell.

Every word felt heavy, as if dragged down by the weight of his own history. He would begin to speak to God, only to stop halfway through a sentence because the memory of Bathsheba's courtyard or Uriah's loyalty or the prophet's voice cut across his thoughts like a blade.

He would then simply sit there—silent, breathing, waiting—hoping that heaven might overlook the smell of smoke rising from the ruins of his soul.

He was still ruling.

He was still functioning.

But internally, he was crawling.

The Night He Finally Fell Apart

The breaking came unexpectedly.

One night, David entered the chamber where the baby had lived for a short time. The cradle was empty. The blankets had been folded neatly and placed aside. No servant dared remove them, as if doing so would erase the memory of the child entirely.

David touched the small wooden frame.

Something inside him collapsed.

He dropped to the floor, the side of his head pressed against the cradle as if listening for a heartbeat that would never return. His shoulders shook. His voice cracked. No words formed—only a sound that had no name. A sound no king had ever made in public, but one many men make in private.

It was the sound of a man whose soul had finally reached its breaking point.

Ashes had become his new language.

He stayed there for hours, curled like a man grieving not only a child, but the person he used to be.

The Psalm That Changed Everything

At dawn, he rose—not with strength, but with surrender.

He walked barefoot to the courtyard where the servants kept ashes for mourning rituals. Without ceremony, without priest, without witness, David stepped into the heap of cold ash.

He scooped it into his hands.

He pressed it onto his head, onto his beard, onto his robes.

He breathed it in.

He let it cling to his skin like a uniform of truth.

Then he whispered the words that would become the spine of his restoration.
Words spoken not from pride, not from survival, but from a heart shattered enough to finally speak honestly:

"Create in me a clean heart, O God.
Not a repaired heart.
Not a less sinful heart.
A **new** heart."

He paused, trembling.

"Renew a right spirit within me.
Not the spirit that once sang for You.
Not the spirit that once killed giants.
Not the spirit that once saw glory rise.
A spirit I no longer possess."

The ash fell from his eyelashes as he blinked.

He continued:

"Do not cast me away from Your presence.
Take the throne.
Take the victories.
Take the songs.
But do not take **You** from me."

His voice cracked on the last word.

Then came the line that defined his return:

"Restore to me the joy of Your salvation."

Not the joy of being king.
Not the joy of being victorious.
Not the joy of being chosen.

The joy of **belonging to God**.

Only that.

Everything else could die.

And much of it would.

But David would not let his soul die with it.

The Repentant King Who Refused to Hide His Shame

When David returned to the palace after that night, he did not wash the ashes from his face.

He walked through the corridors with ash still clinging to his beard.

He sat on the throne with ash on his shoulders.

He met with commanders with ash on his hands.

He judged disputes with ash on his cheeks.

The court watched in stunned silence.

Kings did not show weakness.
Kings did not display private failures.
Kings did not reveal internal fractures.

But David did.

Not to glorify guilt.

But to reveal a truth every ruler tries to hide:

No throne can cleanse a man.

Only God can.

In those days, the people began to whisper again—but this time the whisper was different.

They did not whisper scandal.

They whispered **reverence**.

They had seen kings die without admitting fault.

They had seen kings lie to maintain power.

They had seen kings kill to protect image.

But they had never seen a king seek forgiveness in public, without excuses, without manipulation, without fear of losing authority.

David's repentance did not weaken him.

It purified him.

And because he did not hide his ruin, Israel trusted him again.

The Slow Climb Out of the Wreckage

Repentance did not fix everything.

But it rebuilt David from the inside outward.

He began rising early again—before dawn—praying with a rawness he had not known since the wilderness years. He returned to writing psalms—not to impress, not to lead worship, but to bleed truth onto parchment.

He sought counsel.

He confessed often.

He rebuilt discipline.

He regained humility.

He learned patience.

He allowed grief to become a teacher instead of a jailer.

And slowly—very slowly—the ash on his face was replaced by something deeper:

clarity.

He saw people more clearly.
He saw weakness more gently.
He saw danger more humbly.
He saw sin more honestly.
He saw God more truly.

And the man who emerged from this season was more dangerous to hell than the giant-slayer had ever been.

Because now David did not fight from invincibility.

He fought from **broken purity**.

And broken purity is stronger than innocence.

The Road Back Was Not a Straight Path

There were days when guilt rose again.
Days when temptation whispered again.
Days when loneliness pulled at him.
Days when shame tried to claim his identity.

But now David had a weapon he had never possessed before:

A repentant heart.

A heart that did not hide from God.
A heart that did not lie to itself.
A heart that did not pretend strength.

A heart that did not fear exposure.
A heart willing to kneel at any moment.

This is why repentance is stronger than innocence:

The innocent stand clean.
The repentant **know** why they must stay close to God.

And David would never forget the ash.

Not ever again.

Why This Was the True Turning Point of His Life

David's rise did not make him a great king.
David's victories did not make him a great leader.
David's music did not make him a great worshiper.

His repentance did.

This was the moment when the shepherd became a man after God's own heart—not because he lived perfectly, but because he returned wholeheartedly.

The road back from spiritual ruin had not been easy.

It had been brutal.

But it had brought him home.

Not to a throne.

Not to glory.

But to God.

And that is where David would rebuild his legacy—not through strength, but through surrender.

CHAPTER XVI – The Song of the Child Who Did Not Live

Grief That Never Fully Heals

Some grief arrives like a storm.

Other grief arrives like a shadow that never leaves the room.

The death of David's child did not break him loudly.

It hollowed him quietly.

The palace returned to its rhythm faster than his heart did. Servants resumed their duties. Guards returned to their posts. Councils gathered again. Music returned to the halls. The world, as it always does, continued forward.

But inside David, time slowed to a crawl.

The chamber where the child had spent his few days of breath remained untouched. No one dared enter it unless commanded. And David did not command it. He passed the doorway often, sometimes stopping without realizing he had stopped, staring into the dim stillness within.

There were no sounds in that room now.

No soft breathing.
No infant cries.
No whispered prayers at the bedside.

Only absence.

And absence is the loudest sound grief can make.

David had fasted when the child was alive. He had pleaded with God with his face pressed to stone. He had believed—against hope, against logic—that mercy might yet interrupt consequence.

But it had not.

And now he lived with the strange contradiction that tormenting faith always brings:

He had been forgiven.

Yet the child was still gone.

Forgiveness heals the soul.

It does not resurrect the dead.

The King Who Rocked an Empty Cradle

One night, when the palace slept and the corridors were silent, David entered the child's chamber alone. He closed the door behind him. The moonlight filtered faintly through a narrow window, casting pale lines across the floor and the small, untouched cradle.

He stood there for a long time.

Then, slowly, he lowered himself to the floor and placed one hand on the cradle's edge.

He did not cry at first.

He simply breathed.

And in his breathing was a pain no scream could express.

"I asked You to take me instead," he whispered.
"I was ready to trade everything."

The cradle did not answer.

He rocked it gently anyway.

Not because it would move.

But because memory still demanded motion.

For the first time since the child's death, the truth finally broke through the king's restraint:

This was not only punishment.

This was **mourning without substitution**.

He pressed his forehead against the side of the cradle and finally wept—not as king, not as penitent, but as a father crushed by the one truth no repentance can undo:

Some consequences end lives.

And repentance cannot rewind them.

The Song That Had No Listeners

David sang that night.

But he sang without sound.

His lips moved.

His chest trembled.

His hands tightened and loosened.

Yet no notes left his mouth.

This was the song of a grief deeper than music.

The song of a soul that no longer expects comfort—only endurance.

"I will go to him," he whispered into silence,
"but he will not come to me."

These were not words of despair.

These were words of acceptance.

Acceptance is not peace.

Acceptance is survival without illusion.

David understood that his child was safe.

But understanding does not erase longing.

It only teaches it where to wait.

How the Loss Changed the Way He Fathered

From that day forward, David became a different father to his remaining children.

Not softer.

More haunted.

He bound them with advice more tightly than with affection. He warned before he affirmed. He corrected before he embraced. He feared becoming indulgent—and in his fear, he often became distant.

The loss of one child taught him the fragility of all of them.

But fragility, when handled without tenderness, becomes pressure.

And pressure, when applied to young hearts, eventually becomes rebellion.

David did not see it yet.

But the seed of future tragedy was already pushing through the soil of unaddressed grief.

Why This Grief Never Fully Healed

Some wounds close.

Some scars fade.

But the loss of a child becomes a **permanent chamber in the heart**—a room you no longer enter often, but which is always there.

David would grow older.

His beard would whiten.

His throne would strengthen.

His name would echo through generations.

But this room would never disappear.

He would think of the child during festivals.
During songs.
During laughter.
During moments of triumph.
During moments of quiet.

He would never know what the child's voice might have sounded like.

He would never see his face mature.

He would never argue with him.

He would never bless him as a grown son.

That future had been sealed in fire before it ever breathed.

And no amount of faith could restore a timeline God Himself had chosen to close.

The Strange Peace That Followed the Pain

And yet—David did not drown in despair.

This was the strange holiness of his return to God:

He learned how to grieve without accusing heaven.

He learned how to mourn without poisoning faith.

He learned how to live with loss without demanding that God explain Himself.

That is a higher obedience than victory.

"I will trust You even when You wound me," he whispered once.

Not as accusation.

As surrender.

The Hidden Gift Inside the Loss

Years later, David would understand something he could not understand now:

Had the child lived, that child would have grown under the shadow of scandal, suspicion, and national memory. His very existence would have been a battlefield of whispers.

God had not only judged.

God had also **hidden**.

Hidden the child from shame.

Hidden the child from politics.

Hidden the child from the poison of the throne.

This understanding comforted David later.

But it did not heal him.

Because some losses are not given to us to heal.

They are given to us to carry.

The King Who Learned to Bow in Silence

From that season onward, David stopped asking God questions about death.

He began asking different ones:

"How do I live with what cannot be fixed?"
"How do I love without trying to replace?"
"How do I lead without hardening?"
"How do I sing again without pretending?"

And slowly, he did sing again.

But not with the same innocence.

Not even with the same repentance.

With **reverent sorrow**.

The sorrow of a man who has lost something he will never get back—but who has chosen not to lose God with it.

Why This Chapter Never Ends

This chapter never truly closed in David's life.

It lived inside all the chapters that followed.

Inside every rebellion.
Inside every betrayal.
Inside every failure of his sons.
Inside his reluctance to discipline.
Inside his hesitation to confront.
Inside his fear of losing again.

The song of the child who did not live was never performed.

But it was heard every time David paused a fraction too long before issuing judgment.

Every time his voice softened when it should have hardened.

Every time he hesitated where strength was needed.

This grief did not destroy him.

But it shaped him.

And sometimes, what shapes us is heavier than what breaks us.

CHAPTER XVII – The Psalm of a Father Betrayed

David's Cry When Absalom Rose Against Him

Betrayal always hurts.

But betrayal by a son does not merely wound the heart—

It fractures identity itself.

David had faced giants.
He had faced armies.
He had faced madness on a throne.
He had faced exile, hunger, shame, and death.

But nothing prepared him for Absalom.

The Son Who Was Beautiful and Broken

Absalom was everything the people adored.

Tall.
Striking.
Charismatic.
Flawless in appearance.

From the crown of his head to the sole of his feet, there was no blemish in him. His hair became legend—so heavy and magnificent that it was weighed each year like treasure.

But beauty covered something badly fractured.

And David—wounded by his own losses, softened by guilt, paralyzed by regret—failed to heal what only a father could touch.

Years earlier, David's household had been shattered by violence between his own children. Justice should have come swiftly.

It did not.

David hesitated.

He delayed.

He avoided confronting fully what terrified him most:

His own reflection in his sons.

Absalom watched.

Waited.

And something inside him hardened.

Silence became resentment.
Resentment became ambition.
Ambition became rebellion.

The Son Who Stole a Throne Without Drawing a Sword

Absalom did not rise in violence at first.

He rose in charm.

He stood at the city gate each morning before David's court opened. He listened to grievances. He embraced the wounded. He spoke gentle words to the ignored.

"If only I were judge," he would say softly, "justice would not delay."

The people began to love him.

Not as a prince.

As a savior.

Little by little, hearts transferred their loyalty.

And David… did not see it.

Or perhaps he saw it—

And could not bear to believe his own son would become his enemy.

Then came the message.

"The hearts of Israel have gone after Absalom."

David felt the words strike his chest like a physical blow.

This was not invasion.

This was inheritance turned inward.

The King Who Chose Flight Again

David did not gather his armies.

He did not fortify Jerusalem.

He did not declare civil war within his own blood.

He chose to flee.

Again.

The same king who once fled Saul now fled his own son.

Barefoot.

Weeping.

Ash on his head once more.

As he crossed the Mount of Olives, those loyal to him walked behind in silence. The Ark was brought out by priests, but David sent it back.

"If I find favor in the Lord's eyes," he said quietly, "He will bring me back. If not—let Him do what seems good to Him."

This was no longer strategy.

This was surrender stripped to bone.

From a ridge above, Absalom entered Jerusalem as king.

One generation passing the crown through treachery instead of blessing.

The Father Who Would Not Stop Loving

David could not curse Absalom.

He could not rejoice in the thought of his destruction.

He could not even speak his name without his voice breaking.

The men around him demanded vengeance.

"Let us strike first," they urged.
"Let us crush the rebellion."
"Let us reclaim the throne by blood."

David answered with one command that stunned warriors and advisors alike:

"Deal gently... with the young man Absalom."

Even now.

Even in betrayal.

Even in humiliation.

He was still a father.

And fathers do not easily shift into executioners.

The Battle That David Could Not Watch

When the armies finally met in the forest of Ephraim, David did not join them.

He remained behind.

Walking.

Pacing.

Praying.

Waiting.

The forest consumed more men than swords ever could. Chaos scattered the rebels. Absalom fled on his mule through thick branches.

His famous hair became his undoing.

It caught in the oak.

The king's son hung between heaven and earth—still alive, helpless.

A soldier found him.

And killed him.

When the news traveled back to David, the messenger spoke cautiously, fearing the reaction of a man caught between king and father.

David's first words were not about the battle.

Not about victory.

Not about the throne.

Only one question left his lips:

"Is the young man Absalom safe?"

The messenger fell silent.

David understood.

And his soul collapsed.

The Cry That Shook the Palace

David went up to the chamber above the gate.

He did not sit.

He did not kneel.

He staggered like a wounded man.

And he cried.

"My son Absalom!
My son! My son Absalom!
If only I had died instead of you,
O Absalom, my son, my son!"

His voice echoed through the halls.

The army returned victorious.

But the palace sounded like a tomb.

Men who had risked their lives for their king wept in confusion, ashamed to celebrate a victory that had killed the king's heart.

David's grief was not political.

It was existential.

He had lost:

The son he failed to correct.
The son he failed to heal.
The son he failed to confront in time.

And now the throne he had once fled for righteousness felt like an instrument of execution.

The Psalm That Had No Resolution

This was not a psalm of hope.

Not a psalm of victory.

Not even a psalm of repentance.

This was the psalm of irreversible loss.

"I carried crowns with torn hands,
But I could not carry my own child.
I ruled nations,
But I failed my house.
If this is the weight of kingship,
Let it end with me."

David did not sing this aloud.

But it lived in his eyes from that day forward.

The King Who Returned Broken

David returned to Jerusalem again.

Not as conqueror.

As survivor.

The people welcomed him.

The elders bowed.

The priests sang.

But David's gaze was changed forever.

The throne had taken his son.

And no glory could give him back.

The prophecies spoken long ago were no longer distant warnings.

They had become flesh and death and blood.

And still—God had not abandoned him.

That was the most confusing truth of all.

David had not lost the kingdom.

But he had lost something greater.

And he would carry that loss into every remaining chapter of his life.

CHAPTER XIX – The Psalm of the Broken Throne

The Lament of a Dethroned King

A throne does not break when it is overturned.

It breaks when the one who once sat upon it no longer knows who he is without it.

David had lost Jerusalem.

Not to strangers.
Not to enemies.
But to his own son.

That truth followed him deeper into exile than any soldier ever could.

Each step away from the city stripped another layer from his identity. He was no longer greeted as king. No longer obeyed by command alone. No longer buffered by walls, guards, ritual, and ceremony.

In the wilderness again, there were no courtiers.

Only men who chose to remain.

Only loyalty without obligation.

Only companionship without advantage.

And that was both humbling and devastating.

The First Night Without a Throne

That first night after the flight, David sat beside a small fire far from city lights. The flames were weak. The wood burned poorly. The wind cut cold through torn layers of shame, loss, and exhaustion.

No crown lay beside him now.

No scepter.

No royal bed.

No singers.

No ark.

Only stone, earth, stars, and a few weary men who still called him king even though the world no longer did.

One of the men spoke quietly:
"My lord… what now?"

David did not answer immediately.

Because for the first time in decades, he did not know.

He stared into the fire and felt something unfamiliar settle into him:

Displacement.

The throne had once organized his world.
Now there was only space.

And space can feel like freedom—or like falling.

The King Who Was No Longer Announced

In the days that followed, David began to understand a terrifying difference between his first exile and this one.

The first time, he had been **waiting for the throne**.

Now, he was **waiting to see if he still deserved to return to it**.

Before, the wilderness had trained him in humility.

Now, it tested whether that humility had truly remained with him once power had been tasted.

Villages looked at him differently now.
Some bowed.
Some hesitated.
Some whispered.
Some said nothing.

To many, he was no longer king.

He was a problem passing through their land.

A liability.

A reminder of an unstable Israel.

And David accepted that without protest.

He no longer demanded recognition.

Because he no longer trusted what recognition had once done to him.

The Memory of the Chair That Was No Longer His

At night, sleep came in fragments.

And when it came, it brought dreams of Jerusalem.

He saw the throne room in detail:
The pillars.
The banners.
The carved lions.
The judgment seat.

But when he walked toward it, the chair was always empty.

Or worse—

Absalom sat there instead.

And David would wake choking in the dark, not with fear for his life—
But with grief for a son ruling through deception and bloodless theft.

A throne stolen by charm is more dangerous than one taken by force.

David knew this.

And that knowledge haunted him.

The Lament That No One Dared to Answer

One evening, as they sheltered beside a ravine, David finally spoke to the men—not as commander, but as a broken man naming the reality they all felt.

"I once ruled tribes," he said quietly.
"I now borrow fire."
"I once judged nations."
"I now negotiate for bread."

No one mocked him.

No one corrected him.

They understood.

He continued, his eyes reflecting the flames:

"I do not know if I will ever rule again.
And I will not force God's hand to find out."

That was the lament of the broken throne:

Not defiance.

Acceptance without certainty.

The Psalm That Formed in the Absence of Power

That night, David sang again.

Not as a declaration.
Not as a celebration.
Not as a weapon.

As a surrender spoken into dust:

"I ruled Your people with borrowed breath.
I judged with hands You once steadied.
If the chair I filled now condemns me,
let the ground beneath me teach me truth again."

This was not the song of a fallen king.

This was the song of a man unsure if kingship itself still belonged to him.

The King Who Faced the Possibility of Never Returning

Days passed.

Scouts brought news.

Absalom had fully taken Jerusalem.
He sat in David's seat.
He issued commands.
He was praised by the people.

And for the first time, David considered something he had never truly considered before:

What if he never goes back?

What if exile is not a season—
But an ending?

What if the crown had already passed from him forever?

This question did not ignite fear in him.

It ignited something far worse:

Relief mixed with terror.

Relief that the burden might finally be lifted.
Terror that his life's calling might have been revoked.

It is terrifying to lose your destiny even when destiny terrified you.

The Difference Between Being King and Being Needed

In Jerusalem, David had been obeyed.

In exile, he was needed.

Men came to him not with petitions—but with wounds.
Not with praise—but with questions.
Not with politics—but with fear.

And he discovered something that disturbed him deeply:

He had become a better shepherd since losing the throne.

He listened longer.
He spoke more softly.
He carried burdens he once would have delegated.
He shared food.
He shared watch shifts.
He marched with them instead of ahead of them.

Authority without position is stronger than authority with a title.

David felt this truth forming inside him.

And it frightened him.

Because it meant the throne had never been the source of his kingship.

The Night He Finally Named the Loss

One night, when the camp had grown quiet, David knelt alone in the sand.

And for the first time, he used the word plainly:

"I am dethroned."

Not as a political statement.

As a personal confession.

He let the word sit between him and God without defense.

"I am dethroned.
And I do not know if I deserve to sit again."

The silence that followed was not punishment.

It was space.

And in that space, David understood the central truth of this chapter of his life:

God had not removed him from the throne to destroy him.

God had removed the throne from him to reveal what still remained without it.

The Broken Throne Became a Mirror

The throne had once reflected his success.

Now its absence reflected his soul.

And in that reflection, David saw:

- His strength without applause
- His faith without structure
- His leadership without power
- His prayer without reward

And he saw that, though battered, something in him still stood.

Not the king.

The servant.

Why This Lament Was Necessary

If David had returned immediately, he would have returned unchanged.

But if he returned now—if he returned from a place where even kingship itself had been placed on the altar—

Then he would not rule as before.

He would rule as a man who remembered that the throne is not an achievement.

It is a burden lent.

And burdens may be recalled.

How This Chapter Quietly Changed Everything

From this moment forward, David no longer feared losing power.

Because he had already lost it—and survived.

The broken throne became the anchor of his humility.

He would never again confuse God's favor with permanence.

He would never again confuse blessing with entitlement.

He would never again confuse calling with control.

The throne had shattered.

And in its fracture, David became unshakable.

CHAPTER XX – The Song of the Oak Tree and the Hanging Prince

Absalom's Death and the Collapse of a Father's Heart

Death does not always come as an enemy.

Sometimes it arrives disguised as consequence.

The forest of Ephraim swallowed men that day.

The battle between David's loyal forces and Absalom's army did not rage across open ground where courage could shine and formations could hold. It unraveled in tangled roots, thick branches, and blind panic. The trees became weapons. The shadows became traps. The earth itself turned traitor beneath running feet.

Men died without seeing the blade that ended them.

And somewhere within that chaos, Absalom fled.

No longer the beloved prince.
No longer the admired rebel king.
Now only a young man desperate to escape the machinery of the war he had unleashed.

His mule carried him fast through the trees. Branches whipped at his face. Thorns tore his garments. The sounds of pursuit thundered behind him—shouts, hooves, clashing steel, the merciless breathing of fate itself.

Absalom did not look like a king now.

He looked like a frightened son.

Then his hair caught.

The symbol of his pride—his unmatched beauty, his public glory—became the instrument of his judgment. The thick branches twisted his long hair and lifted him violently from the saddle. The mule ran on without him.

Absalom hung between heaven and earth.

Alive.

Helpless.

The battle thundered past him without noticing at first.

Then a soldier saw him.

Hanging.
Breathing.
Defeated.

The soldier froze.

He remembered the king's command:

"Deal gently with the young man Absalom."

This was no small command.

It was a line drawn between victory and obedience.

The soldier hesitated.

Then he ran to Joab, David's general.

"I saw Absalom hanging in a tree," he said.

Joab looked at him in disbelief.

"You saw him and did not strike him?"

"The king commanded—"

Joab cut him off.

"The king commanded many things," he said coldly.

Then Joab took three spears in his hand and ran toward the place where Absalom hung.

There was no trial.

No speech.

No mercy.

Three strikes ended the rebellion.

Not with judgment.

With finality.

Absalom's body was cut down and thrown into a deep pit in the forest. Stones were heaped over him. No crown. No burial honors. No father's hand closed his eyes.

Only silence beneath stone.

The Messenger Who Dreaded the Truth

When the victory was secured, a messenger ran with desperate speed toward David's camp. Sweat and dust blurred his face. His lungs burned with effort.

David was pacing.

Waiting.

Watching the road with eyes that could no longer see battle—only his son.

The messenger arrived breathless.

"Good news, my lord the king," he said.

David ignored the news every king wants to hear.

"Is the young man Absalom safe?" he asked.

The messenger hesitated.

In that hesitation, David's heart already began to break.

"May the enemies of my lord the king be as that young man is," the messenger answered carefully.

David understood.

Victory collapsed inside him.

The Cry That Shattered the Palace

David turned away from the battlefield sounds—the cheers, the shouts, the footfalls of victory—and walked up to the chamber above the gate.

There was no dignity left in his movement.

Only gravity.

Only weight.

Only death rising into his throat.

He entered the chamber and fell against the wall.

Then the cry tore out of him fully unguarded:

"My son Absalom!
My son! My son Absalom!

Would God I had died for you,
O Absalom, my son, my son!"

This was not grief.

This was **identity collapse**.

He was not mourning a rebel.

He was mourning the child he once held.

The boy who ran through palace gardens.

The son who once sat at his feet.

The child whose hair he once washed with his own hands.

And now that boy was stone-covered in a forest grave.

The king's lament echoed through the halls like a funeral bell that refused to stop ringing.

Outside, the army returned in victory.

Inside, a father's world had ended.

When Victory Feels Like Desecration

The soldiers entered the city quietly.

No songs.

No banners.

No celebration.

They slipped into Jerusalem like men returning from a funeral instead of a battlefield.

They had won.

But their king had lost.

Joab entered David's chamber without ceremony.

"You have shamed the faces of all your servants today," he said bluntly. "You love those who hate you and hate those who love you. You would be pleased if Absalom were alive and all of us were dead."

David lifted his tear-streaked face and said nothing.

Joab continued:

"Now rise. Go speak to your servants. Or this night they will scatter from you, and worse will come upon you than all the evil that has fallen on you before."

The words were cruel.

But they were true.

The king had collapsed.

The nation could not afford for him to remain buried in his grief.

The Most Painful Act of Leadership

David rose.

Not because he was healed.

Not because he was comforted.

But because the people could not survive a king who vanished into sorrow.

He washed his face.

He changed his garments.

He descended and sat again at the gate.

The soldiers saw him.

And slowly, order returned.

But inside David, nothing returned to order.

Why Absalom's Death Destroyed Him More Than All Other Loss

David had lost:

- His child in infancy
- His friend Jonathan
- His mentor Samuel
- His reputation
- His peace
- His innocence
- His throne

But Absalom was different.

Absalom was the living proof that David's personal failure had multiplied into generational ruin.

This was not just tragic.

This was prophetic consequence with a human face.

David did not only bury a son.

He buried the mirror of his own sins.

The Oak Tree That Still Stands

Long after, travelers still whispered of that oak tree.

No one marked it officially.

No monument was built.

No inscription was carved.

But people knew.

A prince had once hung there.

A rebellion had ended there.

A father's heart had broken there.

And David never passed near that region again.

The Song That Could Never Be Sung Publicly

David never wrote this psalm.

It would have destroyed the people's hope.

But it lived inside him in silence:

"I brought him into life,
But could not bring him back from death.
I guided nations,
But failed a son.
If this is the cost of kingship,
let it end with me."

The Truth That Remained After the Death

Absalom's rebellion ended that day.

But David's sorrow never did.

This was not a wound that closed.

This was a wound that aged with him.

Every laugh afterward carried an undertone.

Every celebration held an echo.

Every blessing wore a shadow.

And yet—David lived.

Because grief did not disqualify him.

But it forever humbled him.

And humility is the last crown a king ever wears.

CHAPTER XXI – The Psalm of the King Who Refused to Kill Saul

Power That Chose Purity Over Revenge

There are moments in a man's life when all future kingship, all legacy, all meaning narrows into a single choice.

For David, that moment did not happen on a battlefield.

It happened in a cave.

Long before crowns.
Long before the Ark returned.
Long before the nation sang his name.
Long before Absalom stole his throne and his heart.

It happened when David had every right to kill.

And chose not to.

The Night When Power Lay Defenseless

Saul had hunted David like an animal across wilderness and rock. Not because David had rebelled. Not because he had plotted. But because fear had infected a throne and turned authority into paranoia.

David's men were exhausted from running.

They slept in short fragments.
Ate when they could.
Lived with weapons always within reach.

And that night, hidden deep within a cave, they heard footsteps.

Torches flickered at the entrance.

A lone figure entered.

Saul.

The king who sought David's death had unknowingly walked into the very mouth of his enemy's refuge.

David's men saw it instantly for what it was:

Opportunity.

"God has delivered your enemy into your hands," they whispered.
"This is the moment."
"This is justice."
"This is survival."

David stood motionless against the rock wall.

His pulse thundered in his ears.

The man who had hurled spears at him.
The man who had slaughtered priests for aiding him.
The man who had turned his life into endless flight.

Now stood alone.

Defenseless.

Unarmed.

Unaware.

This was not temptation.

This was **permission wrapped in righteousness**.

And that is the most dangerous form of temptation there is.

When Righteousness Becomes a Weapon

David moved silently through the darkness.

His blade was already in his hand.

Every step forward felt justified.

Every breath whispered logic:

He will kill you if you spare him.
Your men will die because of him.
The kingdom will never be safe while he lives.
This is not murder. This is deliverance.

Saul lowered himself, completely exposed.

David stood a breath away from the end of his suffering.

And then something strange happened.

He trembled.

Not from fear.

From recognition.

He recognized the exact moment when he himself could become Saul.

This was how it begins.

Not with violence as rage.

But with violence as *reason*.

With blood explained as **necessity**.

With murder dressed as **destiny**.

David saw himself in the king he was about to kill—and it horrified him.

He lowered the blade.

Cut only the edge of Saul's robe.

And fled back into the darkness.

His men stared at him as if he had lost his mind.

"You had the throne in your hands," one whispered. "You let it go."

David's voice shook—not with regret, but with spiritual shock:

"I cannot raise my hand against the Lord's anointed— even if that anointed hunts me."

Why This Choice Was Greater Than Any Crown

From a human standpoint, David's choice was irrational.

- Saul would not stop hunting him.
- The threat would remain.
- The danger would grow.
- The kingdom would not come easily.

But from a spiritual standpoint, something far greater than survival was being protected:

David's **inner throne**.

He did not yet sit in Jerusalem.

But that night, he sat firmly in his own soul.

Had he killed Saul, he might have gained a kingdom faster.

But he would have lost the one thing God had been preparing inside him:

Righteous authority.

Anyone can take power by force.

Very few arrive at it without blood on their soul.

The Moment Saul Knew He Had Lost

When Saul exited the cave and reached a safe distance, David stepped out behind him.

"My lord the king!"

Saul turned in shock.

David fell to the ground and held up the torn piece of the robe.

"Why do you hunt me?" he cried.
"Today I held your life in my hand—and I spared you."

Saul's conscience awakened for a moment.

Tears filled his eyes.

"You are more righteous than I," he said. "You will surely be king."

He spoke prophecy with the same mouth that still held murder in its future.

For a moment, the madness loosened.

But only for a moment.

Why David's Purity Terrified Saul More Than Any Sword

Saul feared David's potential kingship.

But what truly undid him was David's **moral refusal to become Saul in order to replace him**.

A man who will not mirror your corruption is the most dangerous opponent of all.

David did not fight Saul.

He outgrew him.

And Saul sensed it.

The Psalm That Was Born from That Night

David never forgot the cave.

It became the private line of separation between the king he would become and the king he refused to be.

The psalm that lived inside him after that night was simple and terrifying:

"I could have killed my enemy.
Instead, I killed the version of myself that wanted to."

This was not weakness.

This was the **refusal to be ruled by fear disguised as justice**.

Why This Choice Echoed Through Everything That Followed

Because David spared Saul, he would later:

- Spare Shimei when cursed
- Spare Jerusalem from civil war
- Spare enemies who later became allies
- Spare even Absalom in his heart, if not in outcome

This moment engraved restraint into his leadership.

Not passivity.

Restraint.

The strength to not become what you fight.

The Permanent Lesson of the Cave

Power that arrives too early destroys.

Power that arrives after restraint **governs**.

David's refusal to kill Saul did not delay his destiny.

It purified it.

He arrived at the throne with clean hands—not because he had never lifted a sword, but because he had refused to lift it when revenge begged him to.

Why This Was David's Most Obedient Victory

He defeated Saul without killing him.

He defeated hatred without absorbing it.

He defeated the shortcut.

And that is why his kingdom endured while Saul's collapsed.

The King Who Learned That Not All Enemies Are Meant to Be Destroyed

Some enemies are meant to be endured.

So that the soul remains uncorrupted.

So that when authority finally comes, it does not arrive poisoned.

David learned that night that the true crown is not gold.

It is **purity under maximum pressure**.

CHAPTER XXII – The Song of the Warrior Who Laid Down the Sword

When War No Longer Brings Peace

There comes a moment in every warrior's life when victory stops tasting like triumph.

For David, that moment did not arrive after a single battle.

It arrived **after too many**.

He had fought giants, Philistines, traitors, rebels, invaders, and even his own shadow. His hands knew the weight of the sword as naturally as they once knew the weight of the harp. His reflexes had been trained in survival so deeply that stillness felt foreign even in peace.

But now, in the later years of his reign, the kingdom stood stable.

Border fires had dimmed.
Trade routes flourished.

Jerusalem had become a city of walls, courts, songs, and sacrifices.

And yet—David grew increasingly restless.

Not with ambition.

With fatigue.

The body that had once run effortlessly across hills now stiffened in the morning. Old wounds ached in cold weather. The scars that once told stories began to whisper warnings.

And inside him, something even heavier had begun to shift:

War no longer brought clarity.

It only brought **echoes**.

The Battle He Should Not Have Fought

One day, news came of a new threat on the frontier. Another uprising. Another enemy rising where an old one had fallen.

The generals gathered.

Plans were drawn.

Weapons were polished.

And as always before, eyes turned to David.

"Lead us," they said.

For years, that call would have ignited him.

This time, it frightened him.

He looked at the map.

At the soldiers waiting.

At the young officers whose faces shone with hunger for glory.

And for the first time in his life, David did not see strategy.

He saw **graves**.

He saw sons who would not return.

He saw mothers who would receive folded garments.

He saw women who would wait for footsteps that would never come.

And he saw his own younger self running into a fate whose consequences he now understood too well.

"I will not go," he said quietly.

The room froze.

"My lord—" the generals began.

"No," David repeated. "Not this time."

There was shock.

And confusion.

And for some—even disappointment.

But there was also something else:

Relief.

For many had learned to fight under David.

But they had also learned to fear his grief.

The Moment He Admitted What War Had Taken from Him

Later that night, alone in the quiet of his chamber, David held his sword across his knees.

Not as a king.

As a man remembering.

He traced the marks along the blade.

Each notch told a story.

Each stain once carried a name.

And now, for the first time, he allowed himself to say the truth aloud:

"I am tired of winning."

Not tired of protecting.

Not tired of defending.

Tired of killing.

He had once believed war was the proof of righteousness.

Now he knew—it was the proof of a broken world.

War had given him a throne.

It had also given him:

- Jonathan's grave
- Absalom's grave
- Uriah's grave
- A child's empty cradle
- A heart that trembled too easily in silence

Victory had not healed any of these.

Why God Would Not Let Him Build the Temple

It was in this season that David finally understood why God had forbidden him to build the Temple.

"You are a man of war," the word had come, years earlier.

At the time, David had felt it as rejection.

Now he realized it was **mercy**.

God had not rejected him.

God had protected the holiness of the house from being built by hands that had carried too much blood.

Not because David was evil.

But because the Temple would need to breathe peace from its stones.

And David's hands had learned too well how to break them.

The King Who Chose to Train Peace Instead of War

From that moment forward, David's leadership changed again.

He still defended Israel.

But he no longer exalted war.

He trained commanders not only to conquer—but to **de-escalate**.

He strengthened walls not to intimidate, but to protect.

He sought alliances before armies.

He sent envoys before spears.

He began to speak openly in council:

"Victory that multiplies enemies is deception.
Victory that preserves life is wisdom."

Some warriors struggled with this.

Others began to breathe again.

The Song of the Laid-Down Sword

One evening, David returned to the place where he kept his first weapons—old slings, worn shields, swords from earlier wars.

He chose one.

The one he had carried longest.

The one that had saved his life more times than he could count.

And slowly, deliberately, he placed it on the stone before the altar.

Not as an offering of defeat.

As an offering of **completion**.

"I will still defend what You give me," he whispered. "But I will no longer worship the battle that once built me."

This was not cowardice.

This was **mastery** over the identity war had once imposed on him.

The Warrior Who Became a Guardian

From that day on, David fought differently.

Not to expand.

To **preserve**.

Not to dominate.

To **protect**.

Not to prove himself.

To **steward what remained**.

He no longer rode at the head of armies.

He rode at the edge of the nation's soul.

Watching.

Listening.

Holding the line between power and peace.

The Quiet Change No One Celebrated

There were no festivals for this transformation.

No songs were written about it.

No monuments were erected.

Because the world honors warriors who **take** more easily than warriors who **stop taking**.

But heaven records different victories.

And this was one of David's greatest:

The day he laid down the sword—not because he was weak, but because he was finally strong enough to live without it.

Why This Was the End of One David and the Beginning of Another

The young David had sung to survive.
The warrior David had fought to protect.
The king David had ruled to stabilize.

Now the elder David would prepare to **transfer**.

Power.

Wisdom.

Responsibility.

And even regret.

Because he finally understood:

Leadership does not climax in conquest.

It matures in **release**.

The Last Line of the Warrior's Song

That night, before sleep, David whispered into the quiet:

"If another generation must spill blood to remain free, let it not be because I taught them to love the blade."

And with that prayer, the warrior finally began to rest.

CHAPTER XXIII – The Psalm of White Hair and Lingering Fire

Old Age, Memory, and Undying Devotion

Old age did not arrive for David like winter.

It arrived like a long evening.

Slowly.

Quietly.

With warmth still in the air—but shadows stretching farther each day.

His hair turned white before his spirit ever cooled. His hands, once fierce in battle and steady on harp strings, now trembled slightly when he lifted a cup. His back ached in the mornings. His sleep grew lighter, broken by dreams that carried more weight than rest.

Yet inside him, something remained unchanged.

Fire.

Not the fire of conquest.

Not the fire of ambition.

But the fire of devotion that had first awakened beneath Bethlehem's stars.

The King Who No Longer Needed to Be Seen

David no longer sat daily in the judgment hall. Younger men now handled the disputes. Advisors debated policies without waiting for his voice. Messengers passed through without urgency.

And David welcomed this.

For the first time in his life, the world did not demand his constant reaction.

He walked slowly through palace gardens.

He sat beneath olives in the afternoon.

He listened more than he spoke.

Children did not recognize him at first.

Then their parents would whisper, "That is the king."

The children would stare in confusion.

This quiet old man?

This was the warrior?

This was the conqueror?

David found strange joy in that.

It meant the image had finally begun to dissolve.

The Nights of Memory

Sleep in old age is different.

It is not heavy.

It is fragile.

David woke many nights with memories standing at the edge of his mind like silent visitors waiting to be acknowledged.

Jonathan's laughter.
Samuel's voice.
The cave's cold stone.
The weight of a severed robe in his hand.
Absalom's face as a child.
Uriah's calm loyalty.
The empty cradle.

Some nights he wept.

Other nights he only stared into the dark.

These were not nightmares.

They were truth returning for review.

And David did not resist them.

He had learned that memory, when faced honestly, finishes the work that time cannot.

The Fire That Still Burned When the Body Could Not

Though his strength faded, his devotion did not.

He still rose early.

Still whispered psalms before the city stirred.

Still lifted his eyes to heaven as he once had beneath shepherd skies.

His prayers were no longer long.

They were distilled.

Not shaped by grand requests.

But by essential hunger:

"Do not leave me familiar with You but absent from You."
"Do not let memories replace Your presence."
"Let my last breath still know Your name."

This was undying devotion.

Not loud.

Not dramatic.

But **unalterably anchored**.

The King Who Felt the Crown Slip Toward the Next Head

David felt it before anyone spoke it aloud.

The shifting.

The subtle realignment of attention.

Solomon's name began to speak louder in the halls.

Not through ambition.

Through inevitability.

David did not resist this.

Because deep within him lived a truth carried since the days of Saul:

Kingship is never permanent.

It is always **temporarily entrusted**.

Yet knowing this truth does not make letting go painless.

The Quiet Loneliness of the Aging King

Even surrounded by people, David felt alone in a way he never had as a hunted man.

In the wilderness, loneliness had been shared.

In old age, loneliness was internal.

His generation was gone.

Samuel gone.

Jonathan gone.

The warriors who had followed him in caves now walked with canes—or not at all.

The young spoke a language that did not fully belong to him anymore.

They revered him.

But did not know him.

And David learned that reverence and understanding are not the same thing.

The Lingering Fire of Repentance

What astonished those few who truly knew him was this:

David never outgrew repentance.

Even in white hair.

Even in stabilizing legacy.

Even in preserved honor.

He still confessed quickly.

Still trembled when conscience touched him.

Still softened when he felt correction rise.

The fire of humility did not burn out.

It purified to the end.

The Night He Returned to the Rooftop Once More

One evening, leaning on a servant for support, David climbed once more to the rooftop of the palace.

The same city.

The same horizon.

The same sky.

But now, the eyes that looked upon it had lived all of it.

He remembered:

Where he had once wandered in silent temptation.
Where he had once tasted forbidden longing.

Where an empire had nearly collapsed inside a single decision.

And now he stood there again.

Not restless.

Not idle.

At peace.

He bowed his head and whispered:

"You gave me back what I tried to destroy.
You kept me when I tried to hide.
You remained when I failed myself.
If this is my final season,
let it still be Yours."

Why the Fire Did Not Go Out

David's devotion survived because it had been:

- Broken by guilt
- Washed by repentance
- Tested by loss
- Stripped by exile
- Strengthened by mercy

- Softened by age

Fire that survives these does not consume.

It illuminates.

The Final Shape of the Man

David was no longer:

The shepherd
The warrior
The fugitive
The conqueror
The rebel
The father in grief
The king in humiliation

He was all of them.

Integrated.

And at last, at rest within himself.

The Last Quiet Song of the White-Haired King

One night, as his breath grew shallow and sleep claimed him earlier than usual, David whispered into the quiet:

"I came with nothing.
You gave me everything.
I return with scars.
You receive me with mercy."

And in that whisper lived the entire story of David.

CHAPTER XXIV – The Song of the House That He Was Not Allowed to Build

The Temple David Would Never Raise

There was one dream that never left David.

Not even in old age.
Not even after crowns, wars, sons, betrayals, repentance, and restoration.

It lived beneath all other visions like a quiet ache:

To build a house for God.

Not a tent.

Not a movable shelter.

Not fabric stretched between poles.

But stone.

Permanence.

A dwelling that would say to every generation:

God does not wander among us as a guest.
He dwells among us as King.

The Night the Desire Was Born

The desire came quietly.

David had finally reached a season of rest. Enemies were subdued. The kingdom stood unified. The Ark rested in Jerusalem beneath its tent. The palace around him rose in carved stone and cedar.

And one night, lying on his royal bed beneath a roof of crafted beams and ornaments, David felt the disparity strike him with unbearable clarity:

"I live in a house of cedar," he whispered,
"but the Ark of God dwells within curtains."

The words disturbed his sleep.

Something felt wrong.

Something felt **disordered**.

He summoned Nathan the prophet the next day and spoke his heart plainly:

"I will build a house for the Lord."

Nathan blessed the thought immediately.

"Do all that is in your heart," he said.

But that night, the word of the Lord came—**not to David, but to Nathan**.

And when Nathan returned the next day, his eyes carried the weight of heaven.

The Words That Shook the Dream

"David," Nathan said gently,
"the Lord says this:

You will not build Me a house.
You are a man of war.
You have shed much blood on the earth in My sight."

The sentence did not explode.

It sank.

David felt the words descend into him like cold rain soaking into dry ground.

He did not argue.

He did not defend.

He did not remind God of victories or devotion or songs or repentance.

He simply bowed his head.

Why God Said No

It was not because David was unfaithful.

It was because he was **too faithful to war**.

Battle had shaped his hands.

Strategy had trained his reflexes.

Blood had followed him into nearly every chapter of his assigned destiny.

The Temple would be a place of peace.

Its stones would absorb generations of prayer.

Its courts would echo with repentance, not battle cries.

Its walls would shelter people who came not to conquer—but to surrender.

And David, the anointed warrior, could not imprint such a sanctuary with hands that had carried too many deaths.

This was not punishment.

It was **boundary born from purpose**.

The Moment He Yielded the Dream Fully

David went alone after Nathan left.

He entered the tent where the Ark rested.

The same presence he had danced before.

The same holiness that had slain and healed.

And there, before the unseen throne, David sat silently on the ground.

Long enough for disappointment to die.

Long enough for pride to fall away without resistance.

Long enough for grief to shape itself into surrender.

"Then let my son build it," he whispered.

The words cost him more than any battlefield ever had.

Because this was not yielding power.

This was yielding **legacy**.

The King Who Prepared What He Would Never Touch

From that day forward, David devoted himself to the Temple in a different way.

Not as builder.

As **provider**.

He gathered materials relentlessly.

Gold.
Silver.
Bronze.
Iron.
Cedar.
Stones without number.

He organized the Levites.

Structured the musicians.

Designed the courses of priests.

Mapped the worship.

Outlined the sacrifices.

Documented the order of praise.

He prepared everything—

Except the final stone.

He would never feel the weight of that mortar.

Never hear the first hammer strike under his authority.

Never walk its completed courts.

Never see the smoke of its first sacrifice rise from the altar.

His fingerprints would be everywhere.

His feet—nowhere.

The Quiet Grief He Never Publicly Named

David never spoke publicly of his sorrow.

But it lived behind his eyes in moments of silent distance.

He had dreamed of standing inside that house.

Of laying the first stone.

Of worshiping beneath a roof raised by his own devotion.

Instead, he would stand outside history's frame—

Forever the father of the Temple, never its builder.

This is a unique grief:

To prepare what you will never enjoy.

To labor for a future that will not include your presence.

To plant trees whose shade your bones will never touch.

And David bore that grief quietly.

Because he understood something deeper than dreams:

Obedience is not measured by what you finish— but by what you are willing to release.

The Conversation He Had with Solomon

One evening, David called Solomon to his side.

The boy—wise beyond his years—sat quietly, listening.

"God chose you," David said softly.

Solomon's eyes widened.

"To build the house I wanted to build," David continued.

There was no bitterness in his voice.

Only truth.

"You will do it in peace," he told him.
"I could only have done it in blood."

Solomon did not speak.

He felt the weight being transferred.

Not only of a kingdom.

But of a holy calling born from another man's unfulfilled longing.

The Spiritual Meaning of the Unbuilt House

David eventually grasped the hidden wisdom beneath God's refusal:

Not every holy desire is meant to be fulfilled by the one who conceives it.

Some visions are seeds.

Some men water.

Some men harvest.

And some men must release everything without ever seeing it completed.

This is the hardest obedience of all.

The Song That Rose from the Unbuilt Stones

Late one night, David walked among the materials piled for the Temple.

Stacks of gold.
Heaps of stone.
Wood cured and ready.

He laid his trembling hand on one of the stones and whispered:

"I will never stand beneath your roof.
But I will stand beneath the God who asked me to let you go."

This was the song of the unbuilt house:

Not the cry of rejection.

The hymn of **completed surrender**.

Why This "No" Was One of God's Greatest Honors

God trusted David enough to say no.

No—to a dream.

No—to a legacy of direct achievement.

No—to eternal recognition as the builder of Israel's most sacred place.

Because God knew:

David's obedience could bear that rejection without corruption.

Only few hearts survive a holy refusal without bitterness.

David was one of them.

The House David Did Build

He did not build the Temple.

But he built:

- A lineage of worship
- A pattern of repentance
- A throne shaped by mercy
- A faith forged through failure
- A legacy where devotion survived at its worst moment

And that house—though unseen—would outlast stone and gold.

The Final Whisper He Left Behind in the Temple's Shadow

In the last season of his life, as plans passed into Solomon's hands and the materials waited for younger strength, David whispered one final truth into the quiet:

"I will dwell in the House of the Lord…
even if I never build it."

And that was enough.

CHAPTER XXV – The Psalm of the Final Anointing

The Last Sacred Sealing

There comes a moment in every chosen life when God no longer tests, no longer corrects, no longer redirects—

Only **seals**.

David had lived long enough to feel that moment approaching.

Not as fear.

As gravity.

The palace moved softly around him now. Servants spoke in lowered voices. Even the guards seemed to walk more gently, as if the air itself had learned to honor the slowing of his breath.

His body weakened daily.

His spirit grew heavier with clarity.

He had outlived his enemies.

He had buried his friends.

He had watched his sons rise and fall.

And now he waited—not for death—but for **completion**.

The King Who Could No Longer Hold the Fire in His Hands

David lay wrapped in layers of cloth to fight the cold that now lived permanently in his bones. No amount of covering warmed him fully. The servants whispered that the fire of his body was fading.

But the fire of his soul burned brighter than ever.

His eyes, though dimming, saw deeper than they had in years.

Every word spoken near him was weighed.

Every intention was sensed.

Every silence spoke its own language.

He was no longer living in time.

He was living in **transition**.

The Weight of an Unfinished Transfer

One burden still pressed heavily on his chest:

The throne must pass.

But how it passed would determine whether Israel entered peace—or another storm.

Adonijah, his elder son, had begun to quietly gather support. Horses, chariots, feasts, alliances. The old machinery of ambition was grinding again.

David was weak.

But he was not blind.

Bathsheba came to him quietly.

Her voice trembled as she reminded him of the oath he had once spoken:

"That Solomon shall reign after me."

David closed his eyes.

The kingdom hung in that breath.

Then he opened them.

And spoke with ancient authority that had never truly left him:

"Bring Solomon to me."

The Moment the Oil Was Prepared Again

The priests moved swiftly.

Zadok prepared the sacred oil.

Nathan stood ready.

The court gathered in trembling silence.

Solomon was brought in—young, uncertain, aware that destiny was unfolding faster than youth ever prepares for.

David looked at him for a long time.

Not as king.

As a father who knew what the throne would cost him.

"I am going the way of all the earth," David said.

"Be strong. Be a man. Keep the charge of the Lord your God."

Then the oil was lifted.

And in that moment, the air changed.

The same oil that had once fallen on David's teenage head now hovered above his son.

Not stolen.

Not rushed.

Not seized by ambition.

But **passed**.

The oil touched Solomon's head.

And the sound of trumpets broke across Jerusalem.

"Long live King Solomon!"

David closed his eyes.

The crown had transferred.

The burden had moved.

The future had begun.

The Final Anointing Was Not Only for Solomon

As the people celebrated outside, something quieter happened inside David.

An unseen oil was poured over him as well.

Not for rule.

For **release**.

All his striving loosened.

All his unfinished guilt softened.

All his hidden regrets exhaled.

This was not forgiveness—he had known that for years.

This was **completion**.

The sealing of a life that God no longer needed to shape.

The King Who No Longer Needed Power to Be a King

David no longer clutched control.

No longer directed strategy.

No longer shaped policy.

But the room still revolved around him.

Not because of the throne.

Because of **weight**.

A weight only time, repentance, loss, obedience, and survival can produce.

Even now—unarmed, uncommanding, fading—

He was still David.

Not by title.

By **substance**.

The Last Psalm That Never Reached Paper

Late that night, when the palace had dimmed and the celebrations softened into distant murmurs, David stirred slightly.

A servant leaned close.

"My lord… do you wish anything?"

David's lips moved faintly.

"Sing," he whispered.

The servant hesitated.

"What shall I sing, my lord?"

David's eyes opened once more.

"Not for me," he said gently.
"Sing for Him."

A simple melody filled the chamber.

Not royal.

Not triumphant.

Pure.

And somewhere inside that fading breath, the last psalm formed without ink:

"I chased nothing that outlived You.
I lost much that taught me You.
If my name fades,
Let Yours remain louder.
If my mistakes are remembered,
Let Your mercy be remembered deeper.
Now seal what You began."

The Final Sacred Sealing

David did not die that night.

But something in him did.

The part that still clung to being needed.

The part that still measured his worth by outcomes.

The part that feared what history might say.

When dawn arrived, the light touched his white hair and his closed eyes.

And for the first time in his life—

David rested without vigilance.

Without fear.

Without anticipation.

Only **trust**.

Why This Was the Most Complete Anointing of His Life

His first anointing made him a promise.

His second anointing made him a king.

This final anointing made him **a finished soul**.

He had been:

- Chosen as a boy

- Shaped as a fugitive
- Crowned as a warrior
- Broken as a sinner
- Restored as a worshiper
- Humbled as a father
- Refined as an old man
- And now sealed as a servant who had run his course

The Quiet Truth That Filled the Room

David had not built the Temple.

Had not saved his sons.

Had not escaped consequence.

Had not ruled without blood.

Had not lived without failure.

But he had done something rarer:

He had **returned**.

Again and again.

To God.

And that was the only finish that mattered.

CHAPTER XXVI – The Song of the King Who Gave His Throne to Solomon

The Surrender of Power

Power is easiest to take.

Power is hardest to release.

David had fought for the throne.
He had fled for it.
He had waited decades for it.
He had bled for it.
He had lost sons because of it.

And now, at the edge of his life, he faced the last and most silent battle of all:

Letting go.

The Throne That No Longer Responded to His Weight

The throne still stood in the great hall of Jerusalem.

Carved lions at its sides.
Polished stone beneath its steps.
Gold dimmed slightly by time.

But David no longer sat upon it as before.

Not because he had been removed.
But because his body could no longer carry what his spirit once ruled with ease.

On the days when he was brought into the hall, supported by servants, the court would fall silent. The elders rose. The commanders bowed. The scribes stopped writing.

The throne still recognized him.

But David no longer **belonged** to it.

He sat there slowly, his breathing shallow, his hands folded, his eyes studying the hall as if seeing it for the last time—which, in truth, he was.

And one morning, as his gaze rested on the empty space beside the throne where a second seat had once been kept for judgment, he understood with piercing clarity:

The kingdom did not need him anymore.

It needed **succession**.

The Quiet Fear of Letting Go

David feared many things in his life.

Goliath had not terrified him.
Saul had not broken him.
War had not silenced him.

But this moment—this moment of surrender—
trembled at the core of every instinct that had once kept him alive:

If I am not king...
Then who am I?

This is the secret terror of all rulers.

They learn to exist as roles.

And one day, the role ends.

David felt it like a physical ache.

Letting go was not weakness.

Letting go was **unmaking the identity he had worn for a lifetime**.

The Kingdom That Trembled Between Two Sons

The danger was deeper than age.

It was political.

Adonijah had risen quietly.

Not in open rebellion—but in celebration.

Feasts were prepared.

Support was gathered.

The machinery of an unauthorized crown was already turning.

The kingdom teetered between two futures.

And David knew:

If I do not speak now, blood will speak later.

The Moment He Chose Solomon Without Apology

When Bathsheba entered his chamber and spoke Solomon's name, David did not hesitate.

Not this time.

Not as he had once hesitated with Absalom.

Not as he had once delayed justice in his household.

He had learned.

He summoned Zadok.

He summoned Nathan.

He summoned Benaiah.

He summoned Solomon.

And with the last unquestionable weight of his authority, he spoke:

"You shall sit on my throne today."

Not tomorrow.

Not after my death.

Today.

This was not abdication.

This was command shaped into release.

The Walk to the Throne Together

Solomon walked beside David through the corridors.

The young man moved carefully.

The old man leaned heavily.

Father and son walked together through power that was already shifting hands as they moved.

The court fell silent.

Solomon stood trembling.

David was helped onto the throne one last time.

And then—

He motioned for Solomon to come closer.

"You will reign after me," David said softly but clearly.
"Not because you are strong.
Not because you are feared.
But because God chose you."

The words did not crown Solomon with greatness.

They crowned him with responsibility.

The King Who Removed His Own Crown

No servant lifted the crown that day.

David lifted it himself.

Slowly.

With trembling hands—not from fear, but from **finality**.

Every memory clung to the gold:

The harp.
The giants.
The caves.
The throne.
The dances.
The sins.
The repentance.
The sons.
The wars.
The tears.

He lifted it from his own head.

And placed it onto Solomon's.

The entire court held its breath.

History shifted.

The Surrender That Broke the Last Chain

In that instant, something invisible snapped inside David.

Not his strength.

Not his loyalty.

But his attachment.

For the first time since his youth, he was not pursuing, protecting, proving, or maintaining power.

He was simply **releasing it**.

And the release was not hollow.

It was holy.

The Father's Final Charge

David leaned close to Solomon.

His voice was weak—but unwavering.

"Serve God with a whole heart.
Do not build your throne on alliances alone.
Build it on obedience.
I failed when I forgot that."

No politics.

No manipulation.

Only truth.

The King Who Stepped Down Without Becoming Smaller

After the crowning, David did not stand.

He was carried.

Not out in humiliation.

Out in honor.

But there would be no return to the throne.

He would never sit upon it again.

Yet something astonishing happened inside him as the power left his hands:

He did not become smaller.

He became **lighter**.

Why This Surrender Was Greater Than Any Victory

David had conquered cities.
Crushed enemies.
Unified tribes.
Expanded borders.

But this—this was conquest over the one enemy all kings eventually lose to:

The self that cannot let go.

Not many rulers surrender while still alive.

Not many step down before death forces the descent.

David did.

And that is why his surrender resounds louder than all his battles.

The Song That Played Beneath the Silence

That night, as Solomon governed his first official day as king, David lay quietly in his chamber.

And in the depth of his chest, a song formed—not of power, not of glory, not of regret:

"I ruled because You gave.
I release because You ask.
I was never the throne—
I was only the breath upon it."

The Truth That Defined His Last Authority

David did not lose his throne.

He **completed** it.

And completion is greater than possession.

CHAPTER XXVII – The Final Psalm Whispered on the Edge of Death

The Last Conversation Between David and God

Death did not come to David as a storm.

It came as a quiet visitor.

It entered the room without sound, without threat, without spectacle. The same way God had first spoken to him in the fields—not with thunder, but with presence.

David felt it before anyone else noticed.

Not as pain.

As thinning.

As if the veil between breath and eternity had begun to soften.

The King Who Knew the Hour Had Come

He woke before dawn.

The room was dim, still wrapped in the blue shadow of early morning. The city beyond his window slept unaware that its greatest king was preparing to leave it forever.

His breathing was shallow now.

Each breath felt like a gift handed to him one at a time.

He did not call for servants.

He did not summon physicians.

He did not seek Solomon.

This moment was not for administration.

This moment was for God alone.

The Silence That Became a Door

David turned his face slightly toward the faint light.

His lips moved.

Not in command.

Not in lament.

In recognition.

"I am here," he whispered.

And in the space that followed, he was not alone.

Not visibly.

Not audibly.

But unmistakably.

The same presence that had walked beside him in sheepfolds, caves, palaces, sin, repentance, war, loss, and surrender was now closer than breath itself.

No throne stood between them now.

No crown.

No failure.

No glory.

Only a man and his God.

The First Words Were Not About Kingdoms

David did not speak of Israel.

He did not speak of Solomon.

He did not speak of the Temple.

He spoke of the beginning.

"You found me when I did not know how to seek You," he whispered.

"I was only watching sheep...
and You were watching me."

Memory was no longer pain.

It was **testimony**.

"I sang to pass the time," he continued,
and You listened as if it mattered.
I fought to survive—
and You turned survival into calling."

His eyes filled with tears that did not fall.

Not from grief.

From clarity.

The Weight of All That Had Been

Slowly, honestly, David spoke through the chapters that had shaped him:

"I feared when I should have trusted.
I trusted when I should have feared.
I killed men and called it duty.
I spared men and called it mercy.
I sinned and tried to hide it.
I returned and You received me."

His voice trembled slightly:

"I lost sons.
I lost friends.
I lost myself at times.
But You never lost me."

There was no defense in his voice.

No justification.

Only truth offered without fear.

The Question He Had Carried for Decades

Then he asked the question he had never dared to fully form until now:

"Was I enough?"

Not for Israel.

Not for history.

Not for legacy.

For God.

The room was still.

And the answer did not come in words.

It came as **assurance**.

Not of perfection.

Of belonging.

David exhaled.

The Confession That Finalized Everything

There was one confession left.

"I loved power longer than I should have," he whispered.
"I loved justice unevenly at times…
But I never stopped loving You—
even when I ran from You inside my own choices."

That truth settled like a final stone.

And peace followed it.

The Last Fear Was Not Death

David was not afraid of dying.

He was afraid of **arriving with unfinished trust**.

But now, trust was complete.

His hands no longer reached for outcomes.

They lay open.

Waiting.

The Final Psalm That Was Never Written

No harp rested beside him.

No scribe waited with parchment.

No priest stood ready.

But still—he sang.

Not aloud.

Inside.

A psalm formed not of words, but of surrender:

"I chased You with songs.
I fled You with silence.
You met me in both.
If I stand before You now without a crown,
let my scars be my offering.
If my name fades in generations to come,
let my return to You remain forever."

The Last Breath Was a Release—Not a Loss

As the sun's first light touched the edge of his chamber, David felt the final breath take shape inside his chest.

He knew it was the last.

Not with fear.

With recognition.

He whispered one final name.

Not his own.

God's.

And then—

The breath went out.

Slowly.

Gently.

Like a flame choosing not to resist the wind.

What the Room Held After He Was Gone

The servants found him moments later.

Still.

Peaceful.

No tension in his face.

No struggle in his posture.

Only rest.

The king was gone.

But **no king had ever left this throne so fully human**.

What Heaven Received That Morning

He did not arrive as conqueror.

Not as warrior.

Not as ruler.

He arrived as what he had first been beneath the stars:

A shepherd.

Carrying nothing.

Owning nothing.

Trusting everything.

And heaven did not receive him by the measure of his victories.

It received him by the measure of his returns.

Why This Final Psalm Was the Only One That Truly Mattered

All others had been sung to express faith.

This one was sung **by faith completed**.

CHAPTER XXVIII – The Eternal Song: The Voice of David That Still Heals the World

David died.

But his voice did not.

That is the great mystery no grave has ever been able to silence.

Kings vanish.
Empires crumble.
Stone collapses.
Names fade.

Yet David still sings.

Not from tombs.
Not from monuments.
Not from history books alone.

He sings from **inside the wounds of humanity itself**.

The Man Who Refused to Become a Legend Without a Heart

Most men who become legends are polished after death.

Their sins are softened.
Their failures edited.
Their contradictions erased.

David was never allowed that luxury.

He remains forever:

- The shepherd and the sinner
- The warrior and the poet
- The king and the broken father
- The worshiper and the man who fell
- The conqueror and the penitent

He stands unhidden in Scripture.

Unprotected.

Unfiltered.

Because healing does not come from perfection.

It comes from **truth that survives shame**.

And that is why David still heals.

Why His Psalms Still Open Human Souls

David did not write from safe distance.

He wrote:

From caves.
From betrayal.
From lust and repentance.
From loss and rage.
From joy and awe.
From exile and return.
From crowns and ashes.

Every human emotion learned to speak through him.

That is why the lonely find him.
The guilty recognize him.
The afraid trust him.

The angry survive through him.
The worshiper rises with him.

David gave humanity **permission to be honest before God**.

And honesty is the beginning of healing.

The Secret Power of a Man Who Keeps Returning

David's greatest miracle was not Goliath.

It was not Jerusalem.

It was not empire.

It was this:

He always returned.

After sin.
After shame.
After grief.
After failure.
After blood.
After collapse.

He never stayed fallen.

That is the eternal medicine inside his voice.

Because the wounded world does not need sinless heroes.

It needs proof that **return is possible**.

Why His Voice Still Walks Hospital Corridors and Prison Cells

David is still sung:

By soldiers shaking in silence.
By prisoners singing through bars.
By widows whispering through tears.
By addicts gasping for one more chance.
By children hiding under blankets in fear.
By churches rising from ruin.

His words reach where theology alone cannot go.

Because they were born where pain actually lives.

The King Who Taught the World How to Cry Without Losing God

Before David, people feared God.

After David, they learned to **cry toward Him instead of away from Him**.

He taught humanity:

- That rage can pray
- That guilt can kneel
- That despair can sing
- That broken hearts still belong in heaven's presence

This is why dictators hate the Psalms.

And why the wounded memorize them.

Why David Still Defeats Giants Today

Not giants of flesh.

But giants of:

Shame.
Addiction.
Hopelessness.
Depression.
Suicidal silence.
Fear of judgment.
Fear of God.

Every time someone whispers:

"Create in me a clean heart…"

A stone flies again.

And another giant falls invisible to history books.

The Crown David Still Wears

David no longer wears gold.

He wears **testimony**.

He no longer commands armies.

He commands **return**.

He no longer rules a nation.

He rules **conscience**.

His throne is now inside human hearts that refuse to give up on God after failing Him.

Why Heaven Still Calls Him a Man After God's Heart

Not because he never sinned.

But because he never hid from God once the truth broke through.

David did not defend himself.

He **opened himself**.

And God does not heal what is defended.

God heals what is revealed.

The Eternal Song Is Not Music

It is not feathered in melody.

It is not confined to instruments.

The eternal song of David is **a posture of the soul**:

"I fall.
I rise.
I return.
Again."

That posture still saves lives.

Why This Book Does Not End with His Death

Because David never truly ended.

He became a **pathway**.

Every soul that finds courage to pray after sin walks **through David**.

Every trembling heart that learns to trust again passes through his shadow.

Every broken believer who dares to sing again borrows breath from his lungs.

What David Knows Now That the Living Still Struggle to Learn

That God never loved him because he was strong.

God loved him because he kept coming home.

And that truth is now released across centuries.

The Last Truth He Left the World

David never said it in these exact words.

But his life carved it into eternity:

"You can fall further than you ever imagined…
and still rise closer to God than you ever dreamed."

The Eternal Song Continues

Every time someone prays the Psalms—

David sings again.

Every time someone repents and rises—

David walks again.

Every time someone broken dares to worship—

David lives again.

Final Closing of the Book

David did not leave a perfect story.

He left a **healing one**.

And the world will need that song until the final human wound is closed.

The Legacy of a King Who Still Sings Through History

David's body returned to the dust long ago.

His throne was claimed by another.
His palace became stone and shadow.
His name passed through scrolls, lips, and centuries.

And yet—

David never truly left.

Because some lives do not end.

They **echo**.

A King Measured Not by Power, but by Return

History remembers conquerors.

Heaven remembers **returners**.

David's legacy was not built on uninterrupted strength. It was built on the courage to stand again after collapse. Empires rise on force. Souls rise on repentance.

David fell harder than most.

And rose deeper than any.

That is why his story survives where so many triumphant rulers become footnotes. His failures were not erased. They were **transformed into doorways** through which millions would later walk toward God without fear.

A Voice That Crossed Centuries Without Aging

Languages changed.

Borders fell and reformed.

Empires swallowed one another.

But David's voice did not age.

Because he never spoke to politics.

He spoke to the human condition.

To fear.
To guilt.
To longing.
To awe.
To rage.
To loneliness.
To hope.

The modern world, with all its speed and science, still feels exactly what David felt in the caves.

And so his words still land where nothing else can.

Why Tyrants Fear David and Broken People Love Him

Tyrants cannot control repentance.

They cannot weaponize humility.

They cannot silence a conscience that sings.

David's legacy is dangerous to every system built on image, intimidation, and perfection. Because David proves that a man can be powerful **and** penitent, crowned **and** broken, chosen **and** in need of mercy.

And that destroys every false god of flawless authority.

But to the broken, David is a companion.

He never speaks from above pain.

He speaks **from within it**.

The Shepherd Who Still Finds the Lost

David began as a shepherd.

And he never stopped being one.

Even now, his psalms walk ahead of the lost, not behind them. They find men and women in midnight hours, in hospital corridors, in prison cells, in grief-stricken bedrooms, in silent despair where no one else enters.

His song does not demand strength.

It awakens it.

The King Who Gave Language to the Soul

Before David, people feared God but struggled to speak to Him with honesty.

After David, the soul learned to talk.

To cry without shame.
To protest without rebellion.
To worship without pretense.
To confess without annihilation.

He gave humanity **permission to be real before God**.

That gift alone reshaped the inner world of millions who would follow.

Why David's Failures Did Not Destroy His Legacy

Because his failures were not his final voice.

Because his repentance was louder than his fall.

Because he never built a theology of excuses.

He built a path back.

And paths back outlast monuments.

The Throne David Still Occupies

Not in Jerusalem.

Not in stone.

Not in gilded halls.

David's throne now exists in:

- The conscience that still trembles
- The addict who still hopes
- The sinner who still kneels
- The orphan who still prays
- The believer who still doubts and still returns

Wherever a human heart whispers, "Have mercy on me, O God,"

David is already there.

Why His Legacy Did Not End With Solomon

Solomon inherited the kingdom.

David left behind the **language of the soul**.

Kingdoms fracture.

Language survives.

Through David, humanity learned how to carry guilt without being crushed by it. How to feel anger without losing God. How to fall in love with heaven without denying earthly wounds.

Solomon ruled an era.

David still shepherds hearts.

The Type of King the World Rarely Sees

The world produces many rulers.

It rarely produces one who teaches how to weep without breaking faith.

David did not rule because he was flawless.

He ruled because he was **reachable**.

And that made him eternal.

The Song That Will Never Finish

As long as humans sin and still hope...

As long as humans break and still pray...

As long as guilt and grace collide inside the same chest...

David's song will not finish.

It does not need a choir.

It does not need a harp.

It rises every time someone dares to say:

"I have failed…
but I will return."

The Last Mark He Left on the World

Not Israel.

Not Jerusalem.

Not conquests.

Not architecture.

But **this truth, carved into history's deepest layer**:

A human being can fall apart completely…
and still belong completely to God.

Final Closing Line

David no longer sings from earth.

But earth still sings because of David.

And as long as that song continues,
the legacy of the shepherd-king will never fade.

Made in the USA
Coppell, TX
20 January 2026

67461690R00144